Walking for Me

Walking for Me
Life Reflections

DANIEL WALSCH

Walking for Me: Life Reflections
Copyright @ 2025 by Daniel Walsch

Cover design by Hannah W. McLaughlin
Cover image adapted from "Man Walking on the Gray Asphalt Road" by Agung Pandit Wiguna via Pexels.com

ISBN: 978-1-942695-46-2

123 Press

123 Press provides support and resources to the George Mason University community for creating, curating, and disseminating scholarly, creative, and educational works.

George Mason University Libraries

4400 University Drive, MS 2FL

Fairfax, VA 22030

www.publishing.gmu.edu

Table of Contents

Introduction	1
Walking	6
Secrets	17
Reality Check	39
Mind Games	49
The Professional Me	68
Family Matters	97
Still Walking	123
Acknowledgements	129
About the Author	131

Introduction

Now in my eighth decade of life, I continue to grapple with the question of me. I have come to know myself to the point I know there remains more to uncover, understand, and even accept. But what also puzzles—intrigues—me is how I got to be me. What shaped me into becoming the person I am? Who can I blame? Who can I thank? Perhaps the quick answer to both questions is "everything and everyone." Having said that, I cling to the notion that there exists a more specific answer. One more detailed and intimate. With this book, I am attempting to chronicle my evolution in the hope a few hints to the answers will reveal themselves. I should also note that I have told my story via sections or topics rather in a more traditional chronological order. Why? Because the telling of my tale in this manner makes more sense to me.

To begin, I do not believe the way I am today is the way I was when I was born. The journey from my beginning to today has been steady but not without zigs and zags and trials and errors. Striking a balance between gravitating toward my own company while dwelling in a world of others. With that, throughout these many years, one thing I can say with confidence—feeling comfort within my own skin—is that I am a classic introvert. I prefer my own company. I do not remember a time when that was not perhaps a defining characteristic. I started that way and here I am still the same. Once an introvert, always an introvert—at least when it comes to me. When one largely dwells in an environment where being viewed as outgoing is judged, generally, with a greater level of acceptance and to be a more positive characteristic, then embracing this truism is no small thing.

My world began and carried forth in a limited way: only child. It evolved to one of what I have come to term "necessary outreach." Nearly everyone possesses and demonstrates introverted and extroverted qualities. We draw on those traits, often, when the situation calls for it. I approach each day by calculating how much energy I will need in my "extrovert tank." When that tank even begins to approach depletion, I immediately begin looking for the nearest metaphoric off-ramp. As part of this self-maintenance I, for one, need to recharge my batteries after—to me—exhausting stretches of time with others. I require time for reflection regardless of whether the company I have kept is large or small in numbers. But on the other hand, at times I confess to gravitating toward openly expressing thoughts and feelings and even feel comfortable when it comes to taking a social risk. Such traits certainly are found in my emotional make-up. Despite that, I very much remain an active member of "team-introvert" even when much of my adult life has been spent in situations where the behavior of an extrovert is needed and even required.

My journey has seen me step into an array of roles: young athlete, where I basked in the attention of others, to news reporter, where I sought out subjects and people to interview, to public relations professional, where I initiated attention for my clients, to being a regular interview subject on an array of television and radio stations, to university administrator, where I had to guide other administrators and faculty members, to university professor, where lecturing before and interacting with hundreds of students was expected. While these roles gave me enjoyment and profound levels of fulfillment, each was also a struggle. Each forced me, if not to turn my back on my innate nature, at least to struggle with going against "my grain." Every day. Looking back on the many parts I have played in life, including that of friend, father, husband and grandfather, two words come to mind: "reinvention" and "continuation." In *On the Origin of Species*, Charles Darwin reflected on the notion that what determines a species' ability to survive is how well they are able to adapt to what he described as their ever-changing environments. Failure to adapt results in extinction. But through adaptation, they continue to move forward, advance and, yes, survive. Each time I was called upon to reinvent myself—whether or not I wanted to—I did. I removed one hat and put on another. Looking back, it is clear that in doing so—leaving one room to enter another—was a continuation. A progression. Yes, I was no longer doing what I had done, but what I was about to begin doing was a logical part of my singular journey: survival.

Through all that, some days were certainly better than others. None, however, were without serious pep talks by me to me. None ended without sighs of relief that I had fooled those around me and, to a lesser extent, myself, once again. How well I did in all this varied. But the fact I did it at all—looking back—was and is good enough for me. I was happy to, at a minimum, skirt by. Anything beyond that was a gift. I remain grateful to have been able to find necessary moments to recharge my emotional batteries. Without them I can, at best, only guess at what my day-to-day lifestyle would be like.

I recognize that I am far from the only introvert who ever had to cope with the rest of world to connect with others, gain an education and earn a respectable living. No doubt all of us that share this characteristic have had more than a mere taste of the challenge of being "on" when internally you are screaming for others to look away so you can go about your own business in your own way with little to no fanfare or notice. In all my years, it has never not been a struggle. In all my years, on some level, I have never not had to fake being extroverted—the opposite of me. It is no wonder then that the simple, usually solitary, act of walking came so readily to me. No wonder it has served as my ultimate sustenance, my escape, my panic room, my chance for reflection, my desired time-out.

This book has been on my mind for years. In my ruminations, several basic questions kept running through my head: What do I want to say? What is my specific story? Why would it be of interest to anyone other than me? What would I want readers to get out of it? Without mercy, the questions gave me pause. Initially, I figured if written well enough, then the text would speak for itself. After all, who doesn't like a well written story? The answer to that, of course, is easy: While folks may appreciate something that is well-written, it does not mean they are going to actually read it any more than admiring a well-mowed lawn will inspire one to cut their own grass. So, assuming for the sake of argument that what I have penned is at least grammatically correct, then so what? Why my story despite the lingering compulsion that I have had to tell it?

Spoiler alert: I am not a famous person. My evolution and existence have not changed the course of history or affected the arc of humankind, as far as I can tell. I do not hob nob with the rich and famous. Nor have I ever. I see myself as a "regular guy" who has moved through his days as best he can. High points. Low points. Mistakes aplenty. Challenges galore. More blessings than I can count. Very much a work in progress even in this eighth decade of my life. If anyone is looking at this book and deciding whether to give it a look-see, then I understand questions such as those that you might be asking yourself right now. Why my story indeed?

Since our birth, we are told that we are "unique." Like nobody else. I believe that to be true but only to a certain point. Those "points" may include our particular perspectives, histories, experiences, choices we make, reactions to the twists and turns of life, our weaknesses and strengths, intensity of our emotions, how we display our emotions, our level of kindness and selfishness, our level of tolerance toward that which we view as being different from us. The list is virtually endless. We may like a good joke, but how we define "good" is part of what distinguishes us. The depth of our many qualities or characteristics and how we exhibit them represent a major part of who and what we are. Those differences, however, do not nullify the reality of our many similarities. In addition to jokes, all of us cry out for acceptance and validation. We seek to be our own person while craving the companionship and even the embrace of others. Undeniably, we are influenced by strangers and family and friends alike.

All of this is most definitely true of me. I am me. Is it possible to be addicted to the physical act of walking? In my case, I will respond in the affirmative. It has been ever-constant throughout my life. Such is the case in this book. Those times I do not specifically allude to it, you can bet I am doing it nonetheless. Walking. Going off on my own. Long walks. Short walks. My acts of desired "me-time." Coupled with that, I am also a composite of all with whom I have encountered, directly and otherwise. The result is me. I am the same person who has trouble remembering where I parked my car at a shopping mall, yet rarely forgets the birthdays of many who are close to me. I value my own space yet need the physical and metaphorical touch of others. I am secure and comfortable in my own skin, yet far more insecure and sensitive to others than I care to admit.

My characteristics are not just mine. My guess is they are shared by most everyone. So, am I truly unique? No. And yet, I am. Just like everyone else. Thus, while this book is my story, it is one in which others can see parts of themselves. In terms of why someone else might wish to read my story, my theory is because they will see reflections of themselves in it. In a global sense, my guess is that many aspects of my story can be found in the stories of others. So, to those giving this book of mine a look-see, you are in here, too. While you may not be mentioned by name, perhaps the mountains which you have had to climb in your life are similar to mine. Perhaps aspects of my tale are found within yours. My story is mine but it also yours only in my case it comes with a twist regarding my ongoing challenge of living life outside of myself. For me, then, one primary take-a-way is that this tale of mine reinforces the notion that none of us is alone. Speaking for myself, that gives me comfort and hopefully it will others, too.

1

Walking

What was it about walking that I liked so much? It would be summer. My parents would be at work. I was home alone. No siblings. Sure, there were other kids in the neighborhood, some of them I even liked and some liked me back. But the prospect of walking for hours without company or conversation was my siren song. "Come on," it would say. "It's a sunny day. Just you and your best friend: thoughts." I could not resist. Nor did I want to. Walking was not a rejection of others. Rather, it was an embrace of greater comfort. Walking was not so much a way of expanding my mind. Instead, it represented an opportunity to enjoy moments without interference or distraction. It fed a kind of awakened addiction within me. Enjoy time but without others. A chance for me to move around in my own space.

So, off I would go. But where? There were woods behind our house. Maybe I could explore them again. Perhaps a journey up and down the many streets of our suburban neighborhood would be interesting? Not different certainly as I had done that many times already. Still, I could go down Summit Avenue, turn onto Kriel Street, and maybe go as far as Gilmore Avenue before turning around and heading back home. Maybe I would see someone I know but not likely. The parents were all at work and their kids were at camp or busy with other things. And if the neighborhood turned out to be empty, I would be fine with that. More time for me and my thoughts. Less pressure to make conversation and be—what? Interesting? Funny?

Entertaining? Not sure. I did not feel as if I was any of those things anyway. But on days like this, that would be okay because I had my thoughts. Give me them and maybe a root beer snowball on a summer day and I would not dare ask for anything more.

Sometimes I would feel particularly ambitious and walk from my house in Woodlawn all the way over to Edmondson Village. One of the great things about that shopping area was its barbershop for kids. In the front window monkeys were housed that provided those of us needing a trim but not really wanting one with great entertainment and—more to the point—distraction. The round trip by foot to Edmondson Village was over three hours. Add in the hour or so I would spend at my favorite drugstore there looking at comic books and magazines, and over half the day would be spent. Was it time well spent? Looking back, I'm not sure. But while it was happening, it felt good. I could not put a price on the inner peace that sprang from such outings. The neighborhood streets would turn into highways. I would have to be on the watch for cars so as not to turn my adventure into more than I bargained for. And suppose something tragic did happen? That was a question I pondered a lot. Would anyone miss me after the first day or two? Would anyone care that I no longer was around? I mean really care? My thoughts and I were not so sure. At the same time, "we" decided not to try and find out even though there were days when it was an agenda item in our one-on-one dialog.

Measuring one's value through the eyes of others is difficult. Someone—like a parent—says "I love you." What does that mean, particularly to one years away from becoming a teenager? To declare love for a child is both profound and abstract. For me, being on the receiving end of such a declaration always felt good and reassuring. At the same time, often I struggled with trying to measure it in tangible terms. It was not like getting change for a one dollar bill. Getting four quarters for that dollar bill made sense. I could hold in my hand those four quarters. "Love," however, was a different story. My mother told me of her love with great frequency. My father, not so much. So, did he not love me? If not, why not? What did my mother see that my father did not? In those early years, I needed to hear the words. They were even more powerful than deeds. Hugs were great. Being covered with warm blankets at night provided great comfort. Being fed every day without fail was nothing less than wonderful. But individually or collectively, for me, each of those and other actions fell short of the spoken word. Even now, well into adulthood, it is those three words—spoken out loud—that have the greatest impact.

That realization makes clear what a disadvantage it was for my father. He was a doer, not so much a mushy, "I love you" type of guy. He was far more comfortable showing his affection via action—even when it came to my mother. On the other hand, my mother was far more at ease with saying those magic words—to me—out loud. I wish I had realized that sooner—like during those formative years while trying to make sense of how I was perceived by those closest to me. I wish I knew exactly how and when and especially why I become a word-person.

Even my own actions, such as walking, came wrapped in a question mark. Yes, I enjoyed doing that. Yes, I looked forward to doing it. And, yes, it gave me pleasure. But how did it connect to my own need for acceptance, self-worth, and security? Whatever the answer to those questions is now, I had no clue back then. The result was a kid not at peace with himself or all that certain with the level or depth of regard others had for him. I dove into the walking-pool because it felt good. At the time, the concept of walking to escape the judgement of others, to reflect on my own developing thoughts or enjoy this act of self-imposed isolation was not clear or even developed.

Still, walking was my "thing." If I was not in the mood to go to Edmondson Village, then heading up to Liberty Heights was worth considering. That was less than a two hour walk from home. While there, I would check out the reading material at its local drugstore and, at the same time, see what movies were playing at the Ambassador Movie Theater located right across the street. Another Jerry Lewis movie? He must make one a week. That was fine by me even though I was not old enough to go alone. I needed my parents for that. Solo movie-going came later.

If I was feeling particularly adventurous, Thursday nights were my opportunity. That was my parents' bowling night. They would be gone about three hours, plenty of time for me to hightail it down to the heart of Woodlawn, the village in Baltimore County where I was raised. What made this trek edgy by my standards was the fact that it was nighttime when I would venture out. Dark. Often I would not walk but run from our front door to my favorite drug store in the heart of the town center. My parents never did learn of these outings. Not from me any way.

Going out like that opened the door to my imagination. The dark side of it. Giving presence to something that was not there before. Between home and my destination, I lost track of the number of shadowy figures I thought I saw. Some were straight ahead while others were next to the homes I passed. What were they thinking? Maybe they did not want any more of me than I did of them. The best way to contend with them was to keep moving forward. Keep running. I only wish that had made my fears go away. But once I hit the town square lights, they disappeared and so, too, did my visions of them. I knew they would be waiting on my run home. I would worry about them then. In the meantime, there were new magazines and periodicals to look at. Maybe a soda to buy and enjoy. Only if I had saved any of the money my mom would sometimes give me.

The figures I envisioned were, of course, only my imagination, images conjured by me. But why were they scary images? Why couldn't they have been images of soft kittens or fuzzy bunnies? Did I imagine these specific ones as a reminder that what I was doing—sneaking out of the house—was directly against my parents' wishes? Or were these demons invented by me for the specific purpose of my overcoming them, to demonstrate to myself just how brave I was? Perhaps a little bit of both. Whatever the specifics, I do recall being genuinely nervous going to and from our house to the town square.

I remember one particular night when my parents arrived home from bowling. Mom was crying. Dad was angry. I dared not come downstairs from my room to find out what was going on. I wanted to know, but a bigger part of me did not. Maybe their friction was about me. I hoped not. It was not the first time I had seen or heard them at odds like this. But this time it felt more intense. Both my parents had tempers, but my father's roar was louder, more threatening. At times when his anger was directed toward me, I would grow extremely nervous to the point I would begin to laugh. Not out of bravado or defiance. More like fear. This would make him even angrier. I only wish I could have controlled my response. The last thing I wanted to do was make the volcano within him even more explosive. Rarely did my mother direct her temper toward me, even if I deserved it. This gave me a feeling of entitlement around her that lasted well into early adulthood. I felt I could say and do most anything around her or even to her without negative consequences. The good news is that gave me a sense of security around my mother that was unique to my relationship with her. Looking back, I can see this was a false reality. The fact is everyone has boundaries. Lines that should not be crossed for fear of triggering pain, hurt feelings, cross words or possible permanent damage. That is a life lesson that I did not come to fully appreciate or embrace till I was older.

    I never did learn the specific reason for my parents' argument. Perhaps it is just as well. In the morning, they both seemed calm. A brave front for my benefit or did they truly resolve their disagreement? I will never know. But at least they were not fighting, so for that I was glad. Whew.

    I never owned a bicycle growing up, so walking was my only option as a way of getting around. I tried learning how to ride a bike but crashed and fell way too often to make this mode of transportation even close to appealing or enjoyable. Sure, all my friends had bikes. I envied how they all could zip around. They seemed so free. So fearless. Good for them. My parents offered to buy me one. But fear always made me answer, "No thanks." Yes, I wanted to ride a bike just like my friends. I wanted to be part of what they did. But the risk of getting hurt and being embarrassed and perhaps judged negatively held me back. While some risks such as running to downtown Woodlawn were ones I was willing to face, riding a bicycle was a "bridge too far" at that point in my life. No amount of encouragement from my parents or friends made any difference.

    If I had had a bike and rode it, what would have happened to me and my thoughts? In all likelihood, riding a bike would have drawn me into becoming one of the pack, one of the kids who traveled the neighborhood rather than the one who could be seen passing on the way out of town on foot. Could I ride a bike and still think about life and its many challenges and imagine life years later as a professional baseball player or rancher or secret agent or sports announcer? Not sure. Too risky. Almost as risky as riding a bike. So, I decided to stick with walking even though part of me wanted to ride. Walking was what I knew. My comfort zone. It served me well and never gave me reason to second-guess myself. My thoughts were my safe place. I was never at a loss for words there. Never had to worry about being judged or disappointing anyone or embarrassing myself. Feeling upset? Misunderstood? Alone? All you need are shoes. Safe place indeed. For a while, I even had a couple of imaginary friends that proved to be great company. When I would talk out loud as I walked along, I felt like I was not just talking to myself. Too bad they never really talked with me. At least out loud. Mainly, when it came to communication, their strengths were in listening. Much like mine. I do not remember exactly when they went away. Did they tire of listening to me? Did I grow bored with them? Maybe the answer to both questions is "yes." Since then, when I'm alone and I talk, it is directly to me.

Funny but it was only later that I began thinking of myself as an introvert. Adults at the time described me as "shy." I probably was. At the same time, however, even that word did not do me justice. I preferred my own company then and generally, still do. The difference now is I am much better at hiding it. As a grown-up, I can engage in chit-chat with the best. Back then, I did a lot of foot-shuffling and looking at anything but the person in front of me. Back then, being alone provided me with the opportunity to peak at the world from behind my own private curtain. Observe. Make mental notes as to what looked inviting and what did not. As a grown up, being alone affords me opportunity to put aside the reality that lives outside me for a bit and construct ways to best contend with it, reflect upon it, make sense of it. For me, being alone was and is a positive aspect of life. It better equips me to put forward the best version of myself to who and all that both surrounds me and of which I am part. That occasional, self-imposed distance, even now, gives me what opportunity I need and crave to study, process and cope. For better or worse, where and what I am now is a direct result of my periodic acts of withdrawal and isolation.

I remember a party that my cousin had at his house for many of his friends. He always seemed so popular—something I envied about him. I remember being surprised that he invited me. Yes, we both went to the same high school, but as he was a year older than me, our social circles were different. The party would give me a chance to hang out with some of his friends, an older, cooler crowd. I arrived. Greetings. Introductions. Me watching the others interact. Joke around. Twenty minutes or so later I was ready to leave. So, I did. No fanfare. No good-byes. I slipped out the front door and walked home. I did feel badly. Letting my cousin down was the last thing I wanted. Would he be hurt? Upset? Maybe. Would he tell his parents? Tell mine? Maybe. All I know is the next time we talked he was cool. Nothing was said about my early departure. For me, another "whew" moment.

As I moved through the final years before college, I kept walking. Yes, I was better at engaging with others. My circle of friends was wider. Yet the invisible shield around me remained intact. Having closer friends was great but still there was that line that only I could see. Only I knew existed. At times others would approach it. Some even took a step or two over it. But inevitably, I would emotionally move them back to the other side of the line.

Years passed and I was in college. University of Tennessee in Knoxville. A journalism major. No car, which wasn't so bad: more opportunities for walking. Around campus. Exploring the city of Knoxville. Up and down Kingston Pike. "Where were you?" was a question frequently asked by roommates. I tried to give them the impression I was a busy guy with a wide network of activities and friends. Neither was true. I even had discovered what I considered to be a secret place on campus to where I could go just to sit and regroup. My own "fortress of solitude." One time I even took a girl there. She was not impressed.

All this walking. All this time with my thoughts. Not much change from my time back home during all those summers, except now I was older. Being away from home at a popular state university with lots of opportunity for parties and displays of school spirit and girls and becoming the person I was to become. Those topics were rarely not at the forefront of my mind. Oh yeah, there was school, too. And classes. The reason I was there. Keeping up with assignments. Studying for tests. Trying to focus on what my parents had sent me there to do. That was not so appealing. Thinking in the abstract was so much easier than processing tangible information and contending with the reality of earning good grades.

I never did get my head around the concept that this time of my life was a golden opportunity to grow intellectually and emotionally and even socially. I never quite connected the dots between the independence of living away from home and advancing into adulthood. The new aspects of my life, from being more on my own than ever before to meeting new people to being more responsible for my own actions, all seemed like singular islands with little connection between them. The fact that they were all painted with the same broad brush is so obvious now. Then, not so much. I was not much of a dot-connector in those days.

So, with all this walking, what did I think about? What great thoughts bounced around in my noggin, particularly in the setting of an institution of higher learning? What gems presented themselves to me that I then turned into action and that led me to unparalleled heights with no missteps, stumbles, shameful acts or outright screw-ups? Just raising that question now makes me smile. The answer is both simple and two-fold: I do not remember and, as best I can tell,

I am still waiting for gems to present themselves much like products coming off a conveyer belt.

The evolution of thought has been dissected by philosophers and scientists throughout the ages. In terms of my own intellectual journey, I have gone from trying to figure out the best ways to integrate the world into my priorities to trying to determine how best I can adjust to the world around me to, presently, looking for the most comfortable ways the world and I can co-exist much like neighbors who share a fence. We are very much part of each other yet not quite one. These days I am content with the universe I have created for myself while at the same time willing to consider ways to expand or, if necessary, further pull-back from all that engulfs me. The thoughts I bandied about in my youth, including years as an undergraduate, no doubt, were far from profound or significant in their singularity. What gives them significance now is their contribution to my specific growth and whatever abilities I developed to make reasonable choices, regroup from setbacks, integrate with others, and, ultimately, survive. The key is to keep moving forward with an open heart and mind. Wherever I might be in my head in these present times is not where I was over a half century ago. I choose to view that as a good thing. Perhaps the best I can say is that my largely forgettable thoughts served as building blocks designed to give me sense enough to grab onto any worthwhile epiphany that might come along. The fact is throughout my thousands of hours of walking and thinking, I was not smart or mature enough to connect dots between all that I did and witnessed and where I might want to go. One might term what I was doing as "processing." If that is true, looking back, I can only conclude that I was and am a slow processor. Why did it seem like most everyone else around me was better at that than I? Why did it seem as if everyone around me had their intellectual and even emotional act together more than I? Surely, there must have been one or two friends that did not have as much on the ball as me? In retrospect, I acknowledge my comparisons with others then were heavily influenced by my own insecurities and negative sense of self. At the same time, that did not make my assessment any less valid or, dare I say, correct.

Mainly, my thoughts consisted of a great many questions. How nice it would be to provide a list of the most profound ones with which I grappled. Few come to mind. One great thing about what transpired in my head during those times is that mostly it was a judge-free zone. Acceptance. Self-acceptance. On the one hand, accepting myself was a good thing. On the other, accepting that I was less-than others was not. Despite that, my inner dialog included ongoing rationalization. To be fair, periodic admonishment. Either way, all about me. Walking also represented a degree of detachment from which I drew comfort. Sure, I was surrounded by plenty of opportunities for engagement. Hanging out with others. Joining clubs. Every so often, I would even do that. Mostly, however, I held back. Not ready to do more than dip my toe in those waters. While walking, I had control. Walking was my wheelhouse. My universe. Crossing the line where others dwelled was a bridge—even at college-age—I was not ready to cross on any kind of sustained basis. When I walked I did so at my own pace. So, it would be until I decided the time was right to cross over to where non-stop engagement, compromise, adjustment and flexibility were the norm.

Prior to college, in high school for lunch, a group of us would always gather at the same table. Our banter made it fun even if my main contribution was listening more than chiming-in. One Monday we all plopped down when someone asked where one of our regulars was. "Oh, didn't you hear?" came the answer. "He killed himself two days ago." We all sat in silence. Stunned. What exactly did that mean? He's dead. He's not coming back? Even now the memory of this unexpected turn leaves me silent. What was going on with Jim that caused him to do that? He was with us all last week just like normal and seemed fine. Was he thinking about ending his life all the while we were joking with each other? Was he weighing how best to end his life when he asked me to switch sandwiches with him? Did he know he was lying when he said on Friday that he would see me the next week?

None of us knew he was so depressed. None of us knew he was quickly approaching a point of no return where death was more appealing than life. Was he giving us signals that none of us saw? The more I thought about it and the more conversation we all heard about Jim, the more the final days of my time with him dominated my thoughts. His death left me with the realization that people—even ones we feel close to—are not always as easy to read as we might think. Maybe because we are close, our close friends try all the harder not to let us in on their deepest thoughts, secrets, fears, demons, etc. Maybe that is what my parents were doing the morning after their bowling night when they came home so upset at each other.

The more I thought about that the more I did not like that possibility. Isn't the whole point of being close to another so you can have someone who gives you near total leeway into their heart and mind? Total access to their thoughts? You can make mistakes, say and do dumb things, yet the ones closest to you accept you just the same with little if any judgement. What a great gift! There is no better safe zone than the sincere embrace of another. Right? So, does this mean you keep the doors to your heart, including windows into your fears and insecurities, open to them? Is not the whole point of closeness knowing what is going on inside the other? Yet, the more thinking I did the stronger came the realization that, yes, people can and do keep secrets from those closest to them. I am not talking about lying about where one really went when they said they were going to the grocery store. Rather, it is about sharing one's inner demons or thoughts or fears or aspirations. How comfortable are we in revealing tidbits like that about ourselves with those to whom we are closest? The only step beyond that, as best I can tell, is being honest with ourselves.

We tend to not always pay attention to signals our ultimate loved-one or BFF might be giving out. We just assume they will tell us if anything deep is on their mind. The result is, at times, they continue to hurt, feel alone, scared, and uncared for. In silence. My friend's suicide planted a seed, one that took years to establish a lasting foothold within me. All of us, especially regarding ones we know the best and love the most, must remain vigilant when it comes to maintaining ties with those to whom we are closest. If this means keeping our own vulnerabilities exposed, then so be it. The best of relationships and even the best of people can never be taken for granted because we can never be totally sure where they are inside themselves. Being close to someone requires vigilance. Warm feelings are the easy part when it comes to friendship and love. Building and maintaining the foundation that allows love and good will to survive is where the real work resides. Without a willingness to expose one's vulnerabilities, then the deepest of wells where love at its most profound dwells remains untapped.

Sharing one's vulnerabilities, I concede, can be off-putting. Being willing to expose one's under belly is not easy to do or digest. Even a simple act of asking another out on a date is such an act. "I like you. Will you spend time with me?" In my junior and senior high school years especially, such an act, to me, was akin to jumping into a swimming pool filled with hungry sharks. Being home at night watching television was so much easier and—yes—emotionally safer. Walking was, too. Walking with others was a big hill to climb for me. To some degree, it remains so.

    I still feel guilty when it comes to my friend's suicide. I feel guilty when one near me is hurting and I fail to notice or pick up on it. Maybe I could have helped ease Jim's burden if I had not been so caught up in me. Even at that age, I had been told that one cannot make others happy until they make themselves happy. Maybe. But Jim's surprising death injected a thought within that I had not had before: our happiness or level of self-contentment should not only be measured by the degree of happiness we bring to ourselves. Rather, the level of happiness we bring to others must be part of the equation. It cannot be a first-me and then-you proposition. The two must be concurrent. A package deal when it comes to fulfilled happiness. Granted, such a formula makes one's happiness that much more difficult to achieve and sustain. But, hey, whoever said being happy was easy, especially when arriving at such a realization that our happiness is not just about us? Others have to be part of the mix. That was and is my take-away from the death of my friend by his own hand. John Donne had it right all along, "No man is an island." One can only go so far when trying to condemn or dismiss wisdom as it applied to happiness. There is a reason why the very best baseball players are the ones who are able to throw, hit, and field rather than just do one of those things well. In the aftermath of the giant shadow of Jim's suicide, I am more convinced than ever that full happiness is the result of balancing one's happiness with that of another or others. Even if we fall short of making both happen, the effort to do so puts one on the path toward full joy. At least that is my lesson learned.

2

Secrets

What we keep hidden from others often reveals as much about ourselves as it does what we share. I say that not as a criticism or even suggestion that many of us possess some type of deep, dark side that would curl the toes of others should our secrets be revealed. For most, I believe, many of our so-called secrets involve past actions that were and would be sources of embarrassment. They are more pieces of information or snippets of our past that we prefer not to share rather than wave like a flag over and say, "Look at this!" We conceal what we conceal to keep others from thinking less of us. We keep hidden aspects of our lives or thoughts we entertain so that others will have fewer reasons to judge us in a negative fashion. We do not want others to even suspect that we fear that which goes "bump in the night." The idea is to encourage others to view us through a positive lens. The irony of that, of course, is it is those vulnerabilities are often what others find most endearing, such as when we have to, metaphorically, open the closet door to see if there really is a monster inside. Never mind our knocking knees.

My knees knock more often than I care to admit. I do not like others seeing my underbelly. I do not like being exposed for not knowing as much as I pretend or understanding as much as I should or not being capable of actions I should be able to perform. Behind the persona I attempt to put forth are rivers of doubt. It is these chinks in my personhood that feed into my introverted nature, my inclination to turn to extended walks so as to avoid confrontation, the potential disapproval of others, and actions on my part that may not go as well as I wish. Yes, walking is a time for reflection for me. I need that. I embrace it. Also, it serves as an act to hide or distance myself—at least temporarily—from that which I do not wish to face or avoid situations where I come across less than those around me.

I have my secrets. My lasting dependence upon the act of walking is a profound one. It provides me with space, helps me achieve clarity, provides me with opportunity to view the choices of others through their lens. Everyone, on some level, has secrets. That we do is understandable and, no doubt, acceptable. Fundamentally human. Nevertheless, secrets can be puzzling as well as hurtful. They can also be lasting to those not allowed to know what they are or are not provided an explanation as to why they are being kept "under wraps." After all, if we all have them and for many of the same reasons, then does it not make sense for us to be more open with each other? In my life, there have been times when I have been kept outside of a person's hidden entranceway into deep areas of their internal world. I confess that it is not something I enjoy even though I fully understand one's hesitancy to being more open. I get it. I wish less of it happened and happens. Taking a leap of faith with each other—trusting people's capacity to accept—would not be a bad thing. Would it?

My own evolution has been shaped by secrets. Their existence, including my own, have long represented a part of life that needs to be more fully addressed. Confronted. Faced-down. This book, to me, represents a step in that direction. My walks: Where did I go? No one knew. Who did I tell about them? Nobody. Did I ever invite anyone along? Nope. They were part of me that I never shared. Looking back, perhaps they were innocent-enough. At the same time, they were profound to me. They represented individuality on my part; a chance to be my own person. In my formative years, as far as I knew, none of my friends took them like I did. To me, they required no justification or defense. I invented them and that was good enough. This chapter puts forward examples of secrets of others that continue to occupy front row seats in my own mind. Without them, I might enjoy greater clarity, more balanced perspective, and courage when it comes to sharing my own history. Or not. With that, as is often the case, I begin with my parents. What was that moment like when my parents met? Was there easy conversation and the sweet discovery people enjoy upon learning they share many likes and dislikes? Were there sparks? Did the smiles between them take on a life of their own with no prompting? Was that occasion a true, "some enchanted evening?" Adding it all up, I choose to answer "yes" because my parents wed approximately one year after first contact.

The occasion they met was a dinner party hosted by my mother and one of her sisters. The sister knew my dad and thought he would be a fun guest. Also, she reasoned, he might be a good person for my mother to meet as mom's social life up till then had been active, yet not fulfilling.

Nellie Lee Martin was raised in Garrison, Kentucky. She was one of thirteen kids. She was, she often relayed to me, the apple of her father's eye. They had a special bond unlike any of her sisters or brothers. I had no reason to doubt her assessment though did question—to myself—if there was not at least one other sibling who also made their father light up. Of the siblings, my mother was closest to her sister, Alma. Yet her favorite in the clan was one of her younger brothers, Jimmy (James Daniel Martin. I was named after him.) Jimmy was the apple of mother's eye even after his untimely death as a young man. Car accident in Florida.

Mom's father ran a general store there in Garrison. My memory of it now is fuzzy though I remember drinking lots of soda whenever we visited. Free soda and candy. What was not to like? Regarding my mother's mother, to call her a housewife does not seem to do her justice. Thirteen kids. Living primarily on the income of her husband. Non-stop laundry, housecleaning, cooking. The father may have been the focus of the family, but my mother's mother was the backbone. My vague memory of him is he seemed kind and gentle. As for the mother, over the years she would visit us in Baltimore, so I had more of a relationship with her. No stories to share, however.

"How did you end up in Maryland?" was a question I revisited with mom over the years. Her story never changed. She moved from Kentucky to Maryland during the Second World War to join her sister, Alma, who was working for the Martin Company in Baltimore (no relation). They lived together for several years and were eventually joined by their youngest sister, Mabel. Three sisters on their own in Maryland. Sounds like a sitcom. All three met their husbands there, had families and never left, except for occasional visits back home. End of story? No. It was not till years later that I learned more details of my mother's biography that gave her persona more depth, color, darkness, substance, and intrigue.

Mom worked at the Martin Company throughout World War II as a kind of Rosie the Riveter. A few years after the war, she took on the job of office manager at Curtis Steel Products, also in Baltimore City. She remained there for over thirty years. It was a happy experience for her as she was respected, well-paid, and much-appreciated by her bosses. Professionally, being a successful career woman was a fact that proved to be a source of genuine and lasting pride for her.

My first paying job was one summer working in the warehouse at my mother's company. I and the other summer helpers would sort sheets of metal. We worked as hard as we needed and not a drop of sweat more. Sometimes I would go up to the main office to see my mother. As a supervisor, she was cordial but cool to those who reported to her. Any deference she showed was to her superiors. Also, she was well organized and efficient. In her overall life, the only thing to which she was more devoted was me. At the time, I thought that was great. Looking back, however, such a reality makes me sad. My father, despite his flaws, deserved better.

My father was born and raised in Baltimore. He was the oldest of three boys, one of whom died at a young age. The other outlived my dad. My dad was named William Herman Walsch. Growing up he was called Bill. But when he enlisted in the Navy, people began calling him Herman or Herm. (Apparently, there were too many Bills in his unit.) My father's father drove a milk truck at a time when milk was delivered to homes much the way mail is today. His mother floated back and forth between odd jobs and being a housewife. They lived in a row house, were not rich by any means but certainly were not destitute. I regret that I have no memory of my father's father. No tales to share. No insights to give. From what I can tell, my father's father was a reliable breadwinner for the family, no small thing for families in the 1920s, 30s and 40s. Regarding my father's mother, one of her final jobs was working concessions at Memorial Stadium, then home of the Baltimore Orioles and Colts. Whenever we would attend games, she would give me a large order of popcorn for free. How I loved that!

This brings me to the point where my parents met. Only a few years difference in age. She from the South, he from just north of the Mason-Dixon line. She was rural. He was urban. From a big family, she had to learn how to pick and choose her battles, how to co-exist, when best to stand-out and when best to keep a low profile. My father, from a much smaller unit, next to the top dog, was the leader. He carried the weight of the family—or felt he did—and grew used to getting his way even if it meant using force. As one of three boys, force rather than negotiation was often the means to an end.

Dad was a veteran. During World War II, he flew for the Navy in the Pacific. Mainly, he and his crew island-hopped. They went where the action was, dad explained. I wish he had shared more with me. I wish I had asked him more about all that he witnessed, endured, had trouble forgetting, and what made him proudest. Occasionally, he would share a morsel of a memory: the helplessness of seeing fellow fliers—friends—shot down. Learning to empty out his shoes every morning for fear that some critter might have crawled inside them during the night. Meeting the actor Tyrone Power.

When the war ended, my father volunteered to extend his tour of duty and help drop leaflets on Pacific islands, letting Japanese soldiers know that there was no more fighting. The war was over. I often wondered if my dad ever kept one of those fliers. I never asked. He did say that he lost several friends during those after-war missions. Apparently, some of the Japanese soldiers either did not believe what was being communicated to them or felt it better to shoot first and then read second. "How did those tragic deaths make you feel?" is one question I wish I had asked.

Generally, my dad kept things close to his chest. He kept many of his thoughts inside. Much of the time, the vibe he gave out—at least to me—was that he was not one to share feelings. Yes, he certainly had them. Anger. Humor. Frustration. Kindness. When they appeared, they did so suddenly rather than make their impending arrival known—much like a batter in the on-deck circle. Perhaps this came from being the "dad" in his family long before he became a real dad. His dad was largely quiet and passive. Upon entering his teen years, more and more my father became his mother's go-to person to deal with her other two sons or to make sure needed chores or repairs around their rowhouse were addressed. My father became an adult at an early age; outgoing when he wanted to be or when the situation called for it. But largely a man within himself. Remote. Not always the best or most sensitive of communicators. A man of great heart, yet resentment, too. He was loved but not always as much as needed, wanted, or felt he deserved. Impatient yet wise. Worldly enough to be comfortable in traveling his own path. I remember asking him why he did not like commercial flying even though he had flown in the most stressful and dire situations during the Second World War. "Because I know what can go wrong," was his reply. Better to do his own thing rather than leave his fate in the hands of others.

Shortly after marrying my mother, he took night classes at the University of Maryland and earned his undergraduate degree in engineering. He landed a job as a draftsman at Westinghouse and worked there until his retirement over thirty years later. I would have loved to have seen him at the office and get a first-hand sense of how he interacted with others. My guess is he was approachable but not overly so. Liked but not beloved. Above all respected.

At the time of his retirement, computers were becoming a regular "tool" for employees. He gave this contraption a try, but quickly decided it represented one trick this old dog did not want to learn. Thus, he decided to retire. Computers were a step outside his comfort zone. With full-time employment in his rearview mirror, dad still had much firepower in his belly to remain active. Not one to embrace idleness, shortly after retiring, he took a part-time job driving a delivery truck. The extra money it brought in was not important. The act of keeping busy and remaining productive were what he embraced.

My father died in November, 1992. Years later, conversations with mom. New information about him and my mother disclosed by her at the beginning of being stricken with Alzheimer's. She was now living with my wife, Jo, and me. While all of us occasionally went out to dinner, part of the routine we established was that I would take mom out for a bite to eat—just the two of us—nearly every week. One time, she began sharing her past with me, including things about my father that I never knew. Secrets.

While still in Kentucky, my mother went to Berea College, a women's institution of higher learning, as a home economics major. It was her first time away from home. In her freshman year, she met a boy. The two began dating and soon went from one to ten on the passion scale. One fateful weekend they sneaked off and got married and then consummated their marriage at some local hotel. At the weekend's conclusion, she returned to campus as if nothing had happened. Shortly afterward, my mother broke the news to her parents. I can only imagine the uproar that ensued. Her parents immediately withdrew mom from college and had the marriage annulled. That was not all. Shortly after those definitive steps, mom was sent away to Maryland to avoid any further contact with this boy. It was then she and her sister became roommates.

How much of this escapade with the boy did my father know? Everything? Nothing? I will never know. It turns out, according to mom, she was not the only one who had been married once before. It seems my father had a sweetheart—a neighborhood girl—before the start of World War II. They married. It was a brief union my mother described in one word: "disaster." The marriage lasted less than a single year. It was hurtful enough to inspire my father to enlist in the Navy and fight anyone he was told to fight.

The fact both my parents had been married once before did not make me think any less of them. People join-together for many reasons. The passion and good intentions at the beginning of any legalized coupling do not guarantee that initial decision will remain strong and viable. People change. So, too, do their interests and feelings. Perhaps more to the point: people find out more about their new partner that gives them serious doubt about their pledge to remain together "till death us do part." As best I can tell, both my parents were driven by fire when they decided to wed their first spouses. The flame within my father seemed to quickly extinguish itself. Thanks to the Japanese government, he was able to end his marriage and put a great deal of distance from his choice very quickly and with no wiggle room. As this was something I never knew about until after my father's death, I can only assume this woman was not dad's great love. Other than being his first wife, I conclude only that her distinction was that she was his first love.

Regarding my mother, others threw water on her flame. My sense is that boy she met in college was her first serious romantic interest. Perhaps it was the crush of shame that led her to give up her young suitor so quickly. Perhaps it was the weight of the great disappointment in her by her parents that drove mom to go quietly into the night or, in her case, agree to relocate hundreds of miles northeast to Maryland. Yes, her favorite sister was there, but up until then, mom had never shared any burning interest in moving out-of-state. But move she did and, according to her, never made any attempt to maintain contact with her young man. I wondered if, in fact, he was her great love. Mom never said.

So, my parents met at a party and the following year—1949—married. Shortly after returning from their honeymoon in New York City, their phone rang. My father answered. A male voice asked to speak to my mother. "Who is this?" my father asked. The man gave his name and then asked my father, "Who are you?" Easy question. "Nellie's husband," my father replied. Click.

It turns out, shortly after moving to Maryland, mom began dating. Even young divorcees, it seems, want to have fun. One man she became extra-friendly with wanted to marry her. One big problem:

he was already married. He also had children. This new suitor was from Brazil where his family lived at the time. He had moved to the United States to find work, with the idea of relocating his family there once had attained regular employment. Somehow, someway he met my mother and the part of his plan of relocating his family soon went out the window. Upon proposing marriage to my mother, he told her of his circumstance. Showing wisdom and restraint, she told him that he had to tell his wife and free himself of his marriage before she would formally consent to his proposal. The man agreed. After all, he was in love.

Their courtship began shortly following the conclusion of the war and into its immediate aftermath. Despite worldwide peace, after over six years of fighting, international travel was not easy or cheap. This was especially true for a young man with little money. The most inexpensive way he could get back home to Brazil was by boat. So, that is what he did. It took months. To further complicate matters, international phone calls were not all that easy back in the 1940s, again, especially, for one with little money. Consequently, the man had little opportunity to talk with my mother while enroute and later, in Brazil while breaking the bad news to his wife and children. It took him approximately one year to settle his affairs and take another boat back to Baltimore. Between the time he left and time he returned, he and my mother had no contact. She, to put it mildly, had moved on. In his absence, mom met, dated, and married my father.

"Whatever happened to him?" I asked mom. She said she did not know but assumed he did not remain in the Baltimore area for long.

In listening to the sharing of this part of her past, I was struck by two things: the story itself of this guy's tragic and failed quest to have eventually taken my mother's hand in marriage; and the ease with which my mother shrugged off all that he went through. No regrets. No guilt. No looking back. Does that classify as being pragmatic? Heartless? I am not sure though few other descriptives come to mind. Perhaps it is an example of my mother's survival instincts and choosing not to be burdened by any second-guessing. After what happened in Kentucky, my mother was going to be the one in-control of her affairs of the heart. Perhaps mom felt that she had given this man from Brazil an assignment that he failed to complete in a timeline that she had determined. The result: he fell short, she moved on, met my father, and that was that.

Fast forward, nearly thirty years later. The season was summer and the day was Sunday. I was married and a young father. I called my mother to ask if my (first) wife, Ida, and our daughter, Tracy, and I could come for a visit. (We lived only a twenty-minute drive away from my parents at the time.) My mother said they were busy, so the answer was "no." Rare was the time that she would decline a visit from us. I learned later that weeks before my mother had received a surprise call from the daughter of her late (and favorite) brother, Jimmy. Until then, no one knew this young adult even existed. It seems as if Jim had had a child out of wedlock. Her birth-father by then had been dead for over twenty years. She reached out to my mother to meet her and any other members of her dad's extended family. Arrangements were made for the Sunday that I had reached out to my mother. I had no idea that this was the "busy" to which she was referring. My parents, two of mom's sisters and their husbands and grown children were invited. Who was not? Me. Learning of this years later, I asked my mother why I was not included. She offered no explanation. At this point, I was not hurt. Just curious. Still am. To me, I found it to be an unnecessary and puzzling secret. Still do.

Looking at the dynamic between my parents, I now see their marriage through eyes that are different than those of a preschooler, teenager or even an emerging adult. Their histories have not changed. It is my perceptions of it all that have evolved. Like them, I have one child. Like them, I have been married twice. The first marriage was to a good person but the love between us did not last. As a couple, we were not strong or wise enough to weather our early storms. That was the case for my parents and their spouses. My second marriage, thankfully, remains viable and strong. Still, I cannot separate my own life experiences from my assessment of my parents as a couple, including the dynamic they created upon having a third person—me—become part of their mix. Nor do I feel I should.

No question, my parents brought considerable strengths to their relationship. They also contributed immeasurably to the formation of me. Everything I became started with them. Certainly in my formative years, they were the yardstick when it came to determining whether I had done well at something. This included my assessment of me. As a youngster, if I was happy, it was largely because of some actions on their part. A nod. A smile. A hug. Words of praise. The same held true for my dark days when I was not feeling so positive about me. My times of depression and self-loathing were usually triggered by their interactions with me. As an only-child, growing up everything, of course, was about me. Test result from one of my classes at school? What did my parents think? Little league baseball game? How did they think I did? Bringing a friend home? What did they think of him and, more broadly, my choice of friends? My parents were the final answer. What they said or how they reacted mattered the most. Carried the most weight. Even more than my reaction. They were my own personal Supreme Court. This was true for my childhood and even through my early years of adulthood. Stepping out from their shadows was not easy. It took me years. Decades. Perhaps longer than most. Looking back, I am not sure if this says more about me or them. Either way, I take responsibility for allowing their level of influence to play with my psyche as much and as long as it did. Yes, I would push back at times. But who was I kidding? In the end, their opinion mattered long after I had "left the nest."

That changed quickly and for good upon the death of my father in November, 1992. Lung cancer. Just like his mother. I was forty-two. Dad was gone and my mother was struggling. In the context of our triad, change was upon us. It was time for our dance to change. That meant new steps from me. There was no discussion about this. No, "Okay. Now what?" moment. I knew and so, too, did mom. It reminded me of an old expression about a son not becoming a "man" until after his father has died. If "man" means being in the driver's seat as to who has final say in family decisions, then that is what happened with me. At least in terms of the relationship with my remaining parent.

One of life's inevitabilities is the moment when the child becomes parent to the parents. Parents age to the point where mentally and/or physically they are no longer able to maintain a life of independence. When that time arrives, generally the child slides into the pilot's seat. In my case, as an only child, it was not a matter of whether this was something I wanted. "The "Walsch flag" needed to be carried. I was the one to do it or it simply would not happen. My accession began, at first, in little ways: checking on mom every day; buying groceries for her; monitoring her bank account; paying her bills; taking care of home repairs; sometimes spending the night at her house if she was feeling uneasy. Eventually, it led to having her move in with my wife, Jo, and me. My wife did not blink an eye about that prospect. Nor did my mother. Mom was happy to hand-over her independence and any level of authority she may have had over to us and me. Again, no discussion. Such a shift did not occur with my father as he aged and became more infirm. Even now, I cannot imagine his putting his life in my hands as easily as my mother did. If he had, I have no doubt it would not have happened without a lengthy stretch of resistance. Much like the fight he made against his cancer. He was a proud man. Giving up the title of "in-charge" would not have come easily to him. Largely for his sake, I am grateful that he never reached that crossroad or that he and I ever had that struggle.

My father and I had a kind of quirky beginning. I was born August 13, 1950, over one month before my actual due date. I weighed less than five pounds. My father was attending a baseball game with my uncle when he received a call that mom was at the hospital and in labor. When he arrived, he shared an elevator with a nurse and a newborn. That newborn was me. Dad did not know my true identify until he followed the nurse and I down the hall to the room where mom was being kept. Any hopes my parents had of having more children were dashed with my birth. Mom's pregnancy was complicated. Plus, she was over thirty years of age. She always said that she was lucky to have had me. My immediate response to that was always, "It was a lucky day for me, too."

Apparently, as I approached my first birthday, I developed great crawling skills. My parents marveled at my ability to scoot, so the story goes. As a result, my father nicknamed me "Skeets." No one else called me that. That was his nickname for me right up to the end of his life. I cherished that nickname. Still do. It represented a special bond between the two of us. About fifteen years after his death, I began a blog on communication. The primary way to access it was and is through its web address: myskeets.blogspot.com.

Some children, I imagine, view their parents as two versions of the same person. From each, the child receives consistency and affection. That was not my experience. My parents were two different people. Hot and cold. Touchy and feely from one and distance from the other. Consequently, with little exception each day I was subject and witness to two sets of behavior. From a general perspective, dad made sure the trains ran on time while mom was the train. Dad set the tone as to how things would play out each day. Mom would then strive to make sure it all happened as it was supposed to. These global roles represented the focus of these two main characters in our three-person play. My parents were the authors and drivers of our unit. I was the recipient. When mom and dad did well, I was the grateful beneficiary. When they both or individually fell short, I felt the victim but not a typical one. Victims, by definition, are not responsible for what is thrust upon them. In my case, I felt responsible. When my parents, either as a twosome or as individuals, were not in sync, rarely did I think, "What's up with them?" Instead, it was more likely "What have I done wrong now?" Is such a mindset unique to children without siblings? Not sure. But I do know it was mine. I took dad's distance personally. I took mom's constant attention personally. From my perspective, how could I not take how they behaved toward me and each other otherwise?

No doubt variations from the daily agenda were necessary and even demanded explanation and attention. Without question, my parents made the called-for adjustments to meet the unexpected twists and turns that define life. I am uncertain how much of those adjustments were ever discussed or formally agreed upon by my parents. I was not privy to that. They simply presented themselves and were accepted. Much like me. Still, whether our days went by as planned or with some variations, the persona of each parent remained constant. Dad was remote. Mom remained a hugger. Dad was, "Throw the boy into the river and let him figure out how to stay afloat. Maybe even swim." Mom was a life jacket. Dad was not one to engage in conversation. Mom was. Dad was not one to offer up many of an "I love you." Mom had an endless supply. I was never sure how dad felt about me at any given moment while there was no doubt with my mother. I tip-toed around dad and danced with mom. Dad seemed to take my company in spurts while mom seemed not to get enough of me. With all that, there was no confusion as to who I wanted to be with more. Mom poured herself into me while dad kept his distance. Loving but in a way that best suited his temperament.

I figured this dynamic emerged as a result of whatever regard each had for me. Not once did it occur to me that their interactions with me were in direct relation to their evolving interactions with each other. We were a triad. Not necessarily a bad thing, but, in our case, a slippery slope toward cracks in the Walsch unit. For it to work, all of us had to have a solid understanding of how it was to progress. That was not the case. I was the one in the dark. I was the one who "did not get the memo." With us, to tap into another cliché, "two's company, three's a crowd" emerged. What was their relationship like before I arrived on the scene? I have no reason to assume it was anything less than upbeat. How much did my arrival change that in a negative way? Without question, my insertion changed the dynamic much like dropping a new fish into a fishbowl with an already comfortable population. Mom gravitated toward me while dad seemed to withdraw. Did mom attempt to obtain emotional fulfillment through her son because she was not getting as much as she needed from her husband? Maybe. Or did she view his feelings as secondary or, worse, expendable? Weekends would arrive. Time off from work. A chance for the three of us to hangout. Do stuff. Except dad took a part-time job as a roofer. Maybe we needed the extra money. Maybe not. He would leave early on Saturday morning and not return till later in the afternoon. That left mom and I without his presence.

Overall, I do not believe dad's distance was a commentary on me. I do not believe he did not love me. I do not believe he ever regretted having a child. Perhaps occasional "misgivings" might be a better way to describe his attitude toward me at times. One female, two males. I was more than a son. I was competition. We both wanted the attention of the female. She viewed the dynamic as one that could be resolved by making a choice. She felt she had to choose. Dad recognized my mother's internal dilemma and made it easier for her. He took several steps back and let her pursue a relationship with me. Subconsciously, did I interpret his choice as a path that I might want to travel one day; being part of something while at the same time being removed or distant? Did I watch him go out the door on his way to embark on his own walks and think, "Hey, I might want to do that someday." Even more, "I will do that someday." Maybe.

At first, with the excitement of having a newborn, this is understandable. The child is brand new. New parents want to be good parents even though they may not know exactly what that means or how it looks. As I was a premature baby weighing-in at less than five pounds, it is possible mom felt overly protective. Was I going to be strong enough to survive my first months? My first year? To make sure I did, mom kept close watch on me. Dad, too, but not in the same way she did. After all, this was the early 1950s. The role of men when it came to contending with babies was different than it was for women. Society said so. So did my parents. Mom hovered. Dad less so. Also, my birth proved to be a difficult one for mom. She was told she could not have any more children after me. Thus, as her only "shot" at parenthood, mom did not want anything to go wrong. Who could blame her?

Dad had his weekend gig, full-time job, and for a while, night classes. Mom had me. No question as to who was going to win the bonding contest. We moved forward with the pattern that my parents had silently set. The pattern of our particular triad began to emerge. Mom and me; and then there was dad. No resistance or arguments. It all seemed natural.

My dad was the ultimate handyman. He always seemed to have one or two projects going on. None were of the replace-a-lightbulb variety. They were complex, time consuming, challenging. Turning our attic into a kind of suite for me that included my own bathroom, bedroom and living room. Building a patio behind our house. Constructing a stone wall in the backyard. None were not impressive. From time to time I would ask dad if I could help. His answer was always a gentle no. "Go see what your mother is doing" is an example of one of his replies. Maybe he sensed I would slow him down. No doubt. More likely, he knew that was not what she would prefer. While it did not automatically mean I would always do things with her, it did mean I was spending less one-on-one time with him.

He liked to take walks. He and our family dog, Checkers, would go exploring in the wooded area behind our house. This was well before those woods were leveled and replaced with baseball fields and a main street. Did I tag along? No. Many times I did ask. Again, I would have slowed him down. Again, he suggested I see what mom was doing. I think I feel more disappointed about that now than I did back then. What did he think about when he took his walks? I wish I knew. Were his thoughts akin to mine when I began taking walks of my own? I wish I had thought to ask. I am not sure if he would have answered truthfully or with anything even close to meaningful detail.

Years passed and the three of us continued along our own paths, mine much more aligned with my mother's. Most Saturdays, she and I would go out to lunch and do some shopping. I can't say I didn't enjoy the attention. Looking back, I can't imagine my company being all that great. Still, off to Hamburgers or Stuarts or Hochschild Kohn's stores we would go. Lunch would be part of the mix. It made me feel so grown-up. Stay home and play with my friends or go out with mom? There was little or no choice. Mom won out almost every time. We would head out in late morning and not return till mid to late afternoon. For mom, it was a good day. Me, too. And maybe for dad as well. Most Sundays involved getting together with family, primarily mom's sisters and their families. At this point, dad has his mother and one brother, who had three kids of his own. We were lucky to see them once each year even though they lived nearly as close to us as mom's sisters. Why was this? Was it because of mom? Dad? I do not know. Another mystery.

The one regular "thing" dad and I did have for several years was going to see the Baltimore Colts play at Memorial Stadium. We had season tickets. This was a time when the NFL played only twelve regular season games, six at home and six away. It was a span of years when the Colts fielded a virtual all-star team week-in and week-out. Lenny Moore, Raymond Berry, Gino Marchetti, Art Donovan, Jim Parker, to name a few. And, of course, Johnny Unitas, the best of the best. Great times, even if at least half the games were played in freezing weather. Dad and I were usually able to keep warm enough. My mind often goes back to those games and those memories.

My dad had a temper. Mom, too, but rarely was hers directed at me. Not surprisingly, dad was the main target of my mother's fury. Did he always deserve it? Not sure. Probably not. Did she when he would verbally blast away at her? Probably not. I do not remember witnessing many big fights between them. Often there would be asides or snide comments. Stretches of silence. Off each would go to their respective corners. I was often nervous around dad because of his temper. There was also the matter of my feeling like I could never please him. It tugged at me. Mom, on the other hand, was easy. Of the two, for a kid with shaky self-esteem, which parent's company I preferred was a no-brainer. And so it went.

And then there was therapy. I was in middle school and showing signs of isolation and depression. My parents decided I should see a counselor. Get professional help. But what did I want? Was I even asked about this? No. I can only conclude my parents believed they knew best. So, arrangements were made. For several months I spent an hour per week talking about me. What else? I cannot remember the therapist's name, but I do recall his staring at me in our sessions with what I felt was unusual intensity. "Does my looking at you make you uncomfortable?" he asked at one point. I said it did and he immediately swerved his chair around so he was now looking at the wall. I remember wondering if this guy was weirder than me. Something else he said at one session that stayed with me was an aside about parents in general: "They are best when kept at a distance." I remember his smiling when he said that. I smiled back though I was merely doing that to be polite. But I believed he was trying to make a point. A good one from his perspective. In retrospect, I believe he felt his comment was spot-on. But, at the moment, I failed to see the relevance of it. After all, it was not as if I was in a position to act on that. That aside, was he suggesting that I begin distancing myself from my parents? Was this a tidbit he wanted me to file away for future reference? Or was this a back-handed way of telling me that I need to be acting more independently? Whatever the point he attempted to make, it changed nothing in my behavior toward my sessions with him and my interactions with my parents. Finally, we reached a point where the doctor felt I no longer needed to keep coming. Whether he believed I was "okay," or had just gone as far as I could, I am not sure. One final session: except this time, it was to be with my parents, not me. Time to add up the score.

It was not till years later that my mother gave me her version of what was said in that final appointment. At the time, neither of my parents shared with me anything that was said. Another secret. Apparently, according to mom, the session turned out to be a reprimand of my father. "You need to lay off him. He is not going to be you!" my mother said the counselor said to my father. Did this mean a victory for my mother? Was this vindication for her? Did this make her the better parent? Were the comments an eye opener for dad? Did the two decide to work together more closely so that I could evolve in a healthier way? "No," to that last question. The result was a greater withdrawing by my father. More home projects. More walks with the family dog. My mother's hovering continued. So, too did dad's outbursts of anger. As for me, my self-doubt did not take a vacation. Not even a long weekend. Nor was my already shaky self-esteem strengthened. I still could not figure out what I was doing wrong in the eyes of my father, but I knew it had to be something.

Settling into my teen years, I wanted a driver's license. Never mind that I did not know how to ride a bicycle. How would I learn? Dad said he would teach me. Isn't that a dad-thing anyway? The lessons were a disaster. I was nervous as hell and he was impatient and quick-tempered. Lots of yelling. Little confidence behind the wheel on my part. One Sunday my parents and I were invited to visit friends. To my surprise, my dad asked if I wanted to drive. I quickly said, "Yes!" A chance to show my stuff. Show that I was ready to take the driver's seat. Off we went: me behind the wheel, dad in the front passenger seat, and mom in the back seat. Within minutes, whatever "stuff" I was showing was making my father extremely nervous. "Slow down…Put on your turn signal…You need to speed up… Watch out for that guy." By now we were on the Baltimore beltway. I could not take it anymore. I stopped the car and said, "You drive." Dad got out to come around and takeover. As soon as I saw he was behind the car, I speeded up and drove away. My mother yelped. I probably went a few hundred yards before stopping so he could rejoin us. What the hell was I thinking? I knew he would be livid. (I was right.) But I was angry, too. A rare act of defiance.

Shortly after that, my parents decided it might be best for me take lessons through a private driving instructor program. I do not recall driving too many more times with my father as a passenger. To complete the story: later that year I too had my driver's test and flunked. (I passed the written part but flopped on the driving part.) Fortunately, I am glad to report, the second time was the charm.

I have often wondered what life between my parents was like after I went away to college and began living on my own after that. Was life better for them? Were they happier? Did they regain their mojo as a twosome? Did they do more things together? Take in a movie? Go out to eat? These are all questions that I never asked of them. I speculated and wanted to believe the answer to them all was "yes." Now looking back, it is also possible they simply carried on with their usual pattern except with me not part of the mix. Old habits and that sort of thing. On the other hand, they did take a trip to Hawaii with a group, including some family members, so perhaps the answer on some level was a soft yes.

Parents are a beginning point for a child; the starting gate. Having only one parent is a setback for a child from the outset. If there are no birth parents, the setback is potentially even greater. In my case, I had two—the requisite number for what many consider to be a healthy start. No guarantees, of course. However, my folks seemed not to be in sync. A fair or equal balance between me and each one did not exist. As a child grows in size, level of maturity, experience and wisdom, they have to set their own path, decide how they will view themselves, how they will behave toward others, how well they will meet their responsibilities, and how they will deal with their own shortcomings, flaws and weaknesses. There is also a matter of honesty toward themselves and others. Once the label of "child" is removed, then all responsibility for addressing each of those questions falls on the once-child-now-adult. The new adult can no longer explain-away their mistakes or misdeeds onto mom or dad. Ideally, mom and/dad teach the child how to cook their own metaphoric soup. What the child does with that information is up to them. How well I emerged into adulthood and dwelt in it because of the lack of balance I had with each parent remains an uncertainty to me. In my case, I had two parents. Lucky me. Even luckier was that both, overall, were good and responsible adults. Did I mention they were both imperfect as individuals and as a twosome? Did I also note that that reality rubbed off on me? My father had a temper and so do I. Is that temper his? No way. It belongs to me. At times, my mother was a champ when it came to passive-aggressive behavior. I am no slouch in that area either. Whose fault is that? Hint: not hers. My father was incredibly selfless at times. Every once in a while I hit that bulls-eye, too. Is that me or him? My mother could be amazingly generous. I have been known to reach out to others in that regard as well. Her or me?

Parents are teachers. They do so in word and deed. They are the ones that all children rebel against, but also spring from. Initially, they are the ones from where we begin setting down the building blocks that define the kind of people we are and age into. Parents teach in ways that are negative and positive. As the child grows, they look at their parents and conclude either, "I want to be like that" or "No way do I want to go that way." Those internal judgements are not often made out loud. But they are definitely thought and made. Definitely acted on, too. Without question, I am a product of my parents. They gave me definition in my early years. Ultimately, I had final say in how I was going to be. My choices, sometimes to my regret, were and are on me. On the flip side, sometimes those choices were positive. That, too, is on me. As two individuals who joined together, my parents taught me much. They were teachers and influential. Perhaps more so than I deserved. I learned from their strengths and weaknesses. I still am. Even now, not a day passes when I do not give thanks to and for them.

A few final thoughts about each...

It was the beginning of Labor Day weekend, 1992. By this time, my first marriage had ended. My ex-wife and I had joint custody of our daughter. This particular weekend she was with her mom. I had just arrived home from work when the phone rang. It was dad asking if he could come over. Of course. Minutes later he was at the door and I could tell he was troubled. With no-build up, he told me earlier that day he had been diagnosed with cancer of the lungs. Doctors did not have much hope that he would survive. I was stunned. Without words. He had none either. Finally, almost as if he were talking to himself, he said, "I plan to fight this as hard as I can for as long as I can." Our eyes teared up. We hugged. Shortly afterward he returned home, leaving me with thoughts and feelings I did not know what to do with. I remember reflecting on a lunch that dad and I had together a few years earlier. I was at a previous job.

Dad called and asked if I wanted to "grab a bite." We had never done that before. We met at a restaurant, placed our orders, and largely sat in silence. Going into it, I had no expectations of either one of us pouring our souls out to each other. There was no need for that, nor any reason to. Just a quick catch-up. Still, that time together haunts me to this day. We had nothing to say to each other. Yet I had a million things I wanted to say, wanted to ask, wanted to share. My job. My future. Marriage. Parenting. The future. I bet he had stuff to toss my way, too. Yet we made small talk as if we were on a blind date where after the first ten minutes each party knew the encounter would be a one-time thing. Did dad initiate our lunch because he had something specific to talk about only to change his mind after seeing how uncomfortable we seemed to be with each other? I hope not. Yet who could blame him if that was the case?

Probably my favorite thing about my father was that he was what I would call a "silent giver." There would be times when places I lived needed repairs, for example, or improvements. Multiple times I would come home to find that they had been fixed, tweaked or made better. I knew who the culprit was. He would take care of it without saying anything or having any expectations of reimbursement or even being thanked. Dad gave love by doing. Not so much by hugs or high praise. When I was much younger, dad would pick me up at the bus stop from school. He always had a treat for me. Again, love by doing. Rarely did he miss any of my little league games or sports activities. No matter how well I may have done, rarely did he compliment me. Yet I was told that he would sing my praises at work the next day. While I wish he had shared his pride more directly with me, it still made me feel good that he was not keeping that pride in his kid to himself.

Years later when my daughter, Tracy, was born, he became more open in displaying affection. When needed, he took her to school in the morning. He initiated quick trips for an ice cream or snowball during the summer, went exploring with her in the backyard. These were just some of the actions he took on her behalf. I loved that he loved her in ways that he did not necessarily show me when I was her age. I loved that she loved him.

Neither mom nor I were present when he died at the hospital. We had been staying with him for days and were told it would be all right for us to go home for the night. The doctors did not expect him to take any kind of dramatic or fatal turn right away. Except he did. They called mom early on a Sunday morning. "Come in now," was their sharp directive. By the time we arrived at the hospital he was gone. We arrived in time to see him there in bed. This vibrant, complex man stilled. The nursing staff was ready to remove the body. We asked for a little time with him. I never asked mom what her thoughts were as she stared at his body. The reality of his passing left her speechless. Me, too. I was nearly as sad at the moment of not being present when he took his final breath as I was at the reality of his actual passing. If only we had arrived a few minutes earlier, then he would not have been alone. I did not miss the irony that at his death once again it was mom and me and then dad on his own.

One of the profound regrets of my life is that I did not speak at his funeral service. Words failed me. The courage to stand before others and share thoughts and feelings that even I had not quite figured out about this man who called me "Skeets" my entire life was absent. Shame on me. Even while sitting in my seat at the service, I felt I was letting him down. Falling short. I was disappointing those who had gathered to celebrate him, too. In my early years, he was an intimidating figure. But more than that, he was also my first hero in life. That crown remains comfortably on his head. Not a day passes when he is not with me. I should have at least stood up and said that.

Part of my reflections about him revolve around the state of his heart in the final weeks and days of his life. Was he okay with life? In adding up his personal score, did he believe he came out ahead? These are more questions I wish I had asked. My sense is his answer would have been "Yes." I sure hope so. Generous people deserve that. My father was a generous man. But instead of gifts from local department stores, he was his gift. His ability to repair light fixtures, paint, shovel the driveway, prepare dinner, read stories to my daughter, and act silly were all parts of his arsenal. He shared them not for recognition but to help. When it came to me, I see him as a first responder. Imperfect? Yes. Flawed? No doubt. A force for good? Damn right. The last thing I ever said to him when he was still coherent was how glad I was that he was my dad. I am forever grateful that he heard me.

The same is true of my mother. I am glad she was my mom. She travels with me every day.

I do my best to honor her innate generosity. She was a "soft touch" when it came to people she loved: me, my daughter, my cousins, their children, her siblings, my wife. Basically, family. She had no problem saying "I love you" out loud. More often, she would express that feeling with shopping sprees and lunches at area restaurants. She always had a smile at-the-ready even if she did not feel like smiling at those around her, including me. There were times when none of us gave her reason to smile. As a child, I would lash out at her if I was angry about something. I could not get away with that with my father, but with mom, it was okay. She would love me no matter what and ride out my bad behavior. She never gave me reason to doubt her devotion. For a child—and adult for that matter—that was her greatest gift.

She lived with my wife and I for the final five years of her life. Her decline and ultimate demise were the result of Alzheimer's disease. The burden of the disease on her psyche and well-being speaks for itself. But the longer she lived with us the more concerned I became at her overall happiness with her life. Was she happy with her life? I think so. Still, memories she would share did not always cast others in a positive light. That included sisters and my father. I can only hope that was the disease talking rather than her heart. I hate to think her final time was filled with that much regret over those closest to her and with whom she spent the most time. Fifteen years after my father's passing at her own end, mom was on a life support machine. I gave the doctors permission to disconnect her. Minutes later she was gone. No pain. At peace. I did speak at her service. In the years between my father's passing and my mother's, I had become more mature. My father's passing had a big hand in that. It and he gave me what I needed to "step up" at my mom's funeral service as well as the ability to move forward even when I did not particularly want to.

My mother and father were good people. Perhaps one benefit of death and the passage of time is that, together, they give one perspective. How I sometimes judged them when they were alive is not how I judge them now. How I judged them then was mostly through my own narrow lens and whatever I may have been experiencing and/or needing at the time. At best, such an assessment is not necessarily fair nor in any way complete. I see that now. For example, what were they thinking whenever I would get mad because I wanted to watch a television program and they did not let me? What was their side of the story? I bet it made a lot more sense than mine. I bet their reasoning to not let me—11 years old at the time—stay at home by myself for ten days while they visited family in Kentucky and Ohio was more solid than was my argument not to go. Maybe—just maybe—they had my best interest at heart more than I gave them credit.

Growing up, I placed my parents high above me. With the passage of time and the reality of my own mortality now beginning to tug at my sleeve, I see them more from an eye-to-eye vantage. Flawed. Inconsistent. Vulnerable. Brave. Reliable. Kind. Individuals who related to and with others in different ways because they were different people. I choose now to focus on the best parts of them and release any other parts that do not support their positives. Parents—even the decent ones—are easy targets to second-guess, criticize, lampoon and disrespect. They are larger-than-life to those of us who are their products, particularly in our early times. Figures that cast wide shadows. Yes, one could argue that persons of such proportion should be knocked down at least several pegs. I agree that ideally their shadows are really not meant for others to live under, but, rather, to emerge from. Yet I did live in their shadows for many years. And, to a certain extent in my own mind, still do. Looking back, growing up, whatever acts of rebellion I exhibited were directed at them. Their actions triggered my reactions. In the case of my father, I never stopped reacting until after his death. In the case of my mother, I never stopped reacting until her physical and mental decline left me with no choice. I am my own adult based on the foundation that my parents helped me construct. I now stand outside the wide shadow of my parents and give what they cast the deepest of appreciation. The best of them resides within me. The rest I have done my best to emotionally shed. For mom and dad, I have no room for anything else.

3

Reality Check

Going for a walk is real. An activity. Perhaps even some degree of achievement. I have always felt good after a walk regardless of the distance, time commitment or how much intellectual contemplating I may have done during it. I was better for having done it. Further, it was acceptable. People ask where you are going and you respond with "For a walk," rarely, if ever, is there a negative reaction. If anything, it is a "Good for you." Athletics was much the same for me, a tangible activity that brought satisfaction, approval and occasional achievement. Looking back, it would be unfair not to acknowledge some positive memories it has given me.

Athletics or sports carried me through nearly the entire first two decades of my life. My natural abilities were a gift. I find myself continuing to give thanks to the memories of my time in competitive athletics. In the eighth decade of my life, I have reached a point where the appreciation for those years I spent participating and competing and, at times, shining in sports to be something I can truly properly embrace. At the beginning, I felt like a champion. In the immediate aftermath of this chapter in my life, I felt more like the opposite. It took me longer than I care to admit to view it all in a more, perhaps, healthy, even-handed way. The journey to my present state has been marked with reflection, regret, denial, celebration, pride, perspective, and, ultimately, acceptance. I see my years as an active athlete as more part of what I needed to hurdle the emotional difficulties of my youth and progress into early adulthood and beyond. Playing sports was my escape. A most fun companion. That aspect of my life where I could say, "Well, at least I can play (fill in the blank)." Sports taught me that old cliché that when life is good, then it is very good. It also taught me the other half of that lesson: fame is indeed fleeting. No question, sports build character in an individual. In my case, it took years—long after I had stopped playing—to come to the realization that character comes from seeing your opponent's hand raised in victory and being able to rise anyway. It taught me that for one to sustain whatever success that one may enjoy in life, it must be the product of consistent effort. It requires commitment. Just as much, I later learned, achievement also demands a solid awareness that success does not just belong to the victorious but also to those who play the game with integrity, honor and love. True success is not exclusively for the one with the trophy on their mantel or even the one with the most talent. Consistent and honorable effort is the key. Studs Terkel once wisely observed that the smartest person is not always the one who has the biggest desk. Yet for part of my youth, I was the one with the biggest desk. I was unable to keep that metaphoric desk, however, because I lacked the maturity to do what was necessary.

One little league team I played on was awful. The Tigers. There was one season where the only time we won was when the other team forfeited the game. I remember our coach, Harry Graham, who also happened to be the neighborhood mail carrier, in one of his postgame pep talks, said what is important is not whether one wins but rather in how one plays the game. Never mind that this statement or philosophy was not coined by Mr. Graham. In the coming years it resonated with me like few others. What the coach was referring to was effort, being the best one can be regardless of what else is occurring around them; living up to one's highest potential despite whatever victories or losses might come their way; doing what one does with honesty and fairness. It took me years to fully embrace what he was trying to tell us and to appreciate how it can be applied to aspects of life that go beyond sports.

I reflect on my time as an athlete with humbleness, an attitude that was more force fed than devoured willingly. I played baseball competitively primarily in my middle and high school years. About eight years after, I had occasion to play in a slow-pitch softball league. The fact I did not know any of the players on my team did not matter. A friend suggested I reach out to one of the players to see if they needed another team member. Sure enough, they did. I saw it as an opportunity of returning to my favorite pastime and perhaps unleashing some of my old magic. As it turned out, the team needed a catcher as its leader had injured his leg and was not able to play that position without discomfort and risking further injury. I happily stepped in. It was a position I had played before and felt I had done well at. Two games later the team leader took me aside and said he was going to go back in and play. A bit surprised, I nodded and sat down on the bench. He was still nursing his injury. For the next few innings I watched him struggle, at times even grimace as he dealt with the discomfort from his still-fresh injury. The rest of the team was very encouraging toward him and seemed to be pleased that he was back on the field.

Obviously, he would have been better off not playing. Yet there he was on the field. And there I was on the bench. None of the players had seen me play prior to joining their team. Their assessment was based strictly on what they were witnessing at that moment. Had I done that badly? Apparently so. Yes, I had some passed balls and poor throws to the pitcher and others. And my hitting was spotty. Still, the regular catcher was injured and I was not. Sitting on the bench watching the action, I quickly added up my own score: those guys would rather have an injured player on the field than me. The blunt answer to my earlier question was, yes, I had not performed well. With that, despite the fact the game was not quite halfway over, I left and did not return. They had made their choice and my feelings were hurt. I was also mad at them. How unfair. It took me several days to accept the reality that my playing had been sub-par and their judgement was sound. Whatever I was before I was not now. The choice the players made was not personal. It was their collective assessment of my playing. Ouch. That taste of humble pie remains everlasting. I had attempted a comeback that proved to be "a bridge too far."

That episode aside, in my years leading up to that experience, what were my sports? Pretty much anything to which I had access, including baseball, basketball, football, soccer, lacrosse, track, and swimming. Baseball was my favorite by far. For what seems like just moments now, I was quite good in all of them. The go-to-guy for my teammates, the player parents urged their sons to emulate, the one element in my young life from which I drew the most pride; that element even my parents pointed at most when talking about me. King of the hill. Top of the heap. A-number one. No question: a heady time. Yes, I had ability. I was well coordinated and not without strength. Was that the result of hard work-out regiments on my part? Strenuous training? Uh, no. For a youngster I physically matured earlier than most of my peers. I was taller and stronger than most. Not bad for a guy who could not ride a bicycle. Sports came easy to me. Sure, I can catch a ball with a lacrosse stick and keep it safely cradled in my stick as I run downfield. Need a goalie for the soccer team? I'm your guy. What's that? The relay team needs one more member for its race? Look no further.

I entered my teens, and life on the field was all roses. My dream of becoming a professional baseball player was on-course. What could go wrong? It was summer. Little league was underway. Another game. I was at bat and connected, sending a rising line-drive between the left and center fielders. I was off to the races. As I headed toward third base the coach seemed to hesitate as to whether I should keep going. I decided to go for it. A vision of another home run flashed before me as I dashed home. The ball reached the catcher—a big kid made bigger with his catcher's mask, shin guards and chest protector—about the same time that I reached home plate. I slid. Ball in his mitt, the catcher pounced. He landed primarily on my right leg. The pain exploded within me. What the hell happened? I slowly rose to my feet and shuffled back to our bench. Our inning was over as I was declared "out" by the umpire. Time to go back on the field. I slowly made my way to the outfield for the remainder of the game. Fortunately, it was nearly over. By the time my parents and I arrived home, my rights knee was the size of a bowling ball. And did I mention that it hurt, too? The next day I was off to the doctor.

It turned out I had torn several ligaments around my right knee. The decision was made to send me to Kernan Children's Hospital, a highly-respected facility located in Baltimore. (Fun fact: Kernan was located directly across the street from where I went to nursery school and kindergarten.) Even professional athletes went to Kernan for rehabilitation. Maybe I would meet some of them. I figured I would be there just a few days. Tops. No one said anything to make me think otherwise. Still, it was scary as I had never been away from home except for an occasional sleepover. Those few days eventually turned into weeks and ultimately a full month. The first two weeks were with the general population. The second two were spent in isolation.

Initially, my stay there was fine. Nothing seemed to be happening other than I was in a strange bed, surrounded by strange people in one of the children's wards. Board games to play. Books to read. Radio to listen to. Television to watch. New friends to make. Still, why couldn't I go home? I kept asking that bottom-line question. It went from day-to-day being unanswered. Time passed. What was the game plan? How long would this continue? The answer came without warning or even a clue as to what form it would take. I woke one morning to find my bed covered red in blood. My blood. A blood clot had formed on my right knee and burst sometime during that night. I freaked out. The staff did their best to calm me. It took them and me a good while. Even longer for me to stop crying. I am sure I did not help the disposition of the other kids in the ward that we were sharing.

I learned later the doctors were not surprised by the development of the blood clot. In fact, they expected it to burst. They were waiting for that to happen. No one had bothered to share any of this with me, however. After that, no one sat me down to explain what was going on and what this meant. The next day I went into surgery. Why? What was going on? Were they going to cut off my leg? I did not know. What I did know was I had been covered in my own blood the day before and was being instructed by anyone and everyone to calm down. My parents were present to send me off to surgery with smiles and reassurances but no information. Typical. Not being as open as I needed them to be. Even a little bit of information would have helped.

The procedure to repair my damaged ligaments went well as the physicians worked their magic and cleaned out the inside of my knee, filling it with tons of gauze held together by metal clamps. Post-surgery, the doctors believed my knee was infected and would be made worse if I was exposed to other patients or they were exposed to me. Consequently, for the next two weeks I was kept in isolation, away from everyone but staff. While there, I remained in bed, enjoyed the attention of the nurses and staff, and learned to become somewhat proficient with navigating bed pans. (A helpful talent to develop but nothing one would put on their resume.) My time in recovery was not total bliss, however. There was a matter of cleaning out the inside of my knee to ensure the healing would proceed without problem and that there would, in fact, be no infection. This meant removing the gauze that was inside me and replacing it with gauze that was fresh and clean. I should have known that procedure was going to be difficult by the fact one morning four nurses entered my room with a doctor. He was there to clean my wound. They were there to assist him. Their job primarily, as it turned out, was to hold me down so the doctor could do what needed to be done. Removing and replacing the gauze was not the only issue. It was those damn metal clamps that made a relatively straight-forward procedure a major and most painful ordeal. The inner part of my skin was very sensitive and raw. As the doctor removed the material inside me, the clamps rubbed against the inside of my skin. Probably the cleaning lasted only a few minutes. My memory, however, is that it lasted hours. These days when asked if there was ever a time in my life when I felt terrible pain, my answer—always—is that morning when my knee was cleaned out after my operation. When it was over, I was assured that the next cleaning would be far less traumatic. And the one after that even less so. And so on. All that, thankfully, turned out to be true.

Finally, two weeks later, I was given the green light to go home. But I would not be able to take up where I had left off with my sports. It would be months before I could even think about that. My right leg was weaker than my left and thus needed time to, in a sense, catch-up. Initially, I would require crutches to get around, thus making it impossible for me to turn to my "old friend:" walking. Before I could even think about returning to that outlet, I first had to enter into physical therapy. The difference in my leg strength had to be addressed. The next school year was now less than a month away. At the time, I was attending a private school that boasted an indoor Olympic-size swimming pool. When not in class, I would be spending my time in the pool using it to help my right leg regain its strength. This continued for the next four months.

Time between my return home and the beginning of the school year went by slowly. It was great being home, of course, but going out and playing would have been great, too. I could not do that. Nor could I even take any meaningful walks. That was frustrating. I liked that. Needed that. I had to return to processing my thoughts outside the context of doing it while exploring my neighborhood on foot. Doable, yes, but not as fulfilling. So, I contented myself with alone time in my room and to enjoying whatever visitors I had and television I could watch. By the time school started up again, I was off the crutches but still not able to get around at any speed other than slow. Yes, this was frustrating, but I did not see my recovery as being less than inevitable. It went as smoothly as I had hoped. I even enjoyed the hours I spent in the pool. Up till then, my swimming had consisted mainly of playing in various public pools. Now I was doing actual swimming. Laps. Add to that my overall health and youth and my recovery was a speedy one. The beginning of the following calendar year found me playing basketball. Baseball season had not yet started. Still, returning to the ball field was never far from my mind.

Minor League, Pony League and Major Leagues—all part of the community baseball program for our county—were my time and place. No hitters. Home runs. All good. All fun. All-star. A few pictures remain of me in uniform. Team photos always found me in the back row because of my height. Between that and my jutting ears, I was easy to find. I was eager to get back into the swing of it all. See old friends and teammates I had not connected with in a while. Regain the imaginary crown I wore proudly on my head. But a funny thing happened on my way to immortality. I was no longer the tall one on the field; nor was I the most graceful one; or the strongest. It seems many of the other kids had caught up with me—some even surpassed—in terms of physical attributes and ability. Their bodies had matured. Their skill level had improved considerably as well. I was still me, while they were much better versions of how I remembered them. They could now hit the ball. Throw far. Throw hard. Run fast. Not just in baseball. Other sports as well. In fact, more and more of my peers could do those things as well if not better than me. I was like an aging athlete only I did not have the excuse of age. What happened? Was it possible that they had advanced while I stood still? Whatever the reason, my fall from being number one—in my mind—happened quickly. Fortunately, the only one who seemed to appreciate my athletic decline was me. This unexpected turn only escalated for the remainder of my middle and high school years. It was a new landscape that caught me off guard. I did not see it coming. I was now just another member of the team. Little more. Yes, I was on various varsity and junior varsity teams. But being just a member is not nearly the same as being the headliner.

It did not help that I suffered more injuries after the experience that resulted in me being in the hospital for a month. On different occasions I suffered serious sprained ankles; first the right and then the left. Pulled muscles in my back. Back to the crutches. Even a back brace for a spell. Recovery each time was only for a few weeks, but, to my mind, this was valuable time lost.

When college came along, I was able to disappear because that is what high school graduates did. This also includes athletes of high school age who were not good enough to advance to sports at the collegiate level. I say that not as some self-depreciating statement designed to garner sympathy or pep talks. Simply, it is a statement of fact. Playing sports in college was something most kids I knew did not do, so the fact that I was one of them was no big deal. Never mind that I lacked the skill set to be even considered for baseball or any other sport at that level. So much for standing out. So much for having that one area of my life that for others to see me they had to look up. At best, they could see me eye-to-eye or even by looking down. What I call my "walking reflections" took on a dark tone. Self-doubt blossomed but not in any way that a flower does that results in enjoyment or, more to the point, peace of mind. My walks brought me little solace because there seemed to be little within from which to draw. Being older, I knew more was expected of me. Yet I sensed I was not coming through the way I at least did on the ballfield. My walks now were more of an escape than they were opportunities for deepening my level of self-awareness and identifying strategies to achieve positive experience.

Welcome to the new reality. Academically, I was, at best, still average. Introverted, too. Far from being a ladies' man. Far from being a big man even in homeroom. Sports was the one area where I distinguished myself. That disappeared. The thought of my sitting on the bench under any circumstance was unimaginable. As my junior and senior years in high school progressed, my sitting on the bench during games became the norm. I remember one basketball game when our team was down by over thirty points and still the coach did not give me any play-time. Outwardly, I pretended not to mind. Inwardly, however, it was a different matter. There are few things worse than having one's feeling of mediocrity validated. There was now not a single area in my life where I did not feel that way.

With the conclusion of my time in high school I turned away from sports. I began turning away from whatever thrill of competing I had. For me, the disappointment within me was too great to do otherwise. Yes, I could have redoubled my efforts to train, seek to improve my skills. No question I had talent. It was a solid foundation on which to raise myself to a level from which I could possibly pursue a respectable career. After all, during high school, college recruiters did check me out. One summer I even played for a lower level farm team as part of the Atlanta Braves organization. The potential was there. Instead, mentally, I walked away. Physically, too. This included not even watching sports on television, reading box scores or keeping up with the latest stats. Oh, once in a while I would attend a live sports event. It was still fun. Only different. Sports at the University of Tennessee, my undergraduate college, is a big deal. I found Saturday afternoon while everyone was at the football games was a great time to do my laundry. No competition. Good time to go walking, too.

Yet…Yet….Yet…In my mind, I persisted in seeing me in a way that was counter to how I felt others viewed me. I was a good athlete! As good as ever, dammit! I screamed inside my head. Time passed and the screams lessened. The belief in my abilities lessened. Acceptance of my new reality slowly but steadily made itself at home in my head and heart. It was just a matter of time before it became a permanent resident.

One day while hanging out with some friends in college, one asked why I never talked about my own time at playing football, baseball, etc. in high school. I just shrugged. "Not much to tell, really," was my answer. By then, whatever success or highlights in me that dominated my memories were already being erased. Fading away. They were already on their way out the door with me holding it. This was by choice. Silly to ignore reality. It was time to chart other courses. With luck, perhaps I would find one that would ring my bell the way throwing a good curveball did, the way hitting a twenty-footer did, the way catching a pass did.

Sports had carried me from my very early years to the beginning of my adulthood. Now it was time for some other "thing" to take over. But what?

Even as I gradually but steadily distanced myself from the part of my life that gave me the most sense of worth, I did not see its departure as tragic. Or even sad. I refuse to now. Simply, I view myself as one of the thousands of youngsters who played sports but grew up to do other things. At the time, I looked at my self-assessment as a simple matter of recognizing and embracing reality. Seeing what is rather than what I wanted to see. My own internal drama. This did not leave me heartbroken as much as it did rudderless. Compass anyone? Well, maybe a little of it left me sad. One might call it grieving, with a dash of disappointment in myself. What young boy does not dream of a whirlwind life in sports at least some time in their young lives? I sure did. I defined myself through sports. That no longer was the case as much as I wanted it to be. The definition of me had been erased but not replaced.

Postscript. One summer afternoon, still in college, I was on a public bus with my cousin riding home from some event. Two guys, a little younger, sitting in front of us were talking about their times playing baseball in Woodlawn. Our ears perked up as this was part of our history, too. Unexpectedly, one of the guys said to his friend, "There was this guy Danny Walsch who was awesome. He could do anything!"

Even now the memory of that singular moment rings in my ears. It was like a major injection of pride except instead of in one of my arms, it went right into my heart. Perhaps my glory days really did have some glory in them after all. Perhaps some of my achievements had brought rays of sunshine to the lives of others. Who knows for sure? But it sure is nice thinking that might be the case.

4

Mind Games

I "got" walking right from the get-go. Connecting the dots between my intellectual musings while doing it and what I was experiencing beyond my walks was another matter, however. That took decades. Much like a boxer who sees an opening in his opponent's defenses yet is not able to take full advantage of it. Where to begin?

First grade. At military school!?! No way. Not that there is anything wrong with that, of course. But for me, in terms of physical and mental acuity, not a good fit. Men and women who do have that have the "right stuff." I did not. I lacked signs of intellectual maturity or a sense of direction. So, following successful experiences at nursery school and kindergarten, where did I spend the first eight years of my education? That's right. Military school. McDonogh School, a private school in Baltimore County. Founded in 1873, it was organized as an all-white, all-boys, semi-military academy. When I arrived there in 1956, it was still all-white, all-boys, and semi-military.

My parents wanted the best for me academically. Their choices were public school where all my neighborhood friends were going or a private school whose academic programs were considered to be superior to that of most public schools in the entire state. McDonogh, I admit, had a great deal more to offer than my local elementary school. There was horseback riding, swimming, after school athletics, a football team with its own stadium, and a ton of athletic fields on which to play and enjoy. Plus, if all went well, I could attend classes there all the way through twelfth grade. One stop shopping. I was five years old when my parents took me out there to attend an open house. Even I could see there was no comparison between what our local elementary school had to offer versus McDonogh's menu. I eagerly said I wanted to go to McDonogh. My parents seemed pleased. The admissions officer seemed pleased. And I was pleased for helping make them all pleased, a rare achievement for most anyone my age. Certainly for me.

At the time, I was even thrilled at the prospect of wearing a uniform every day. If that wasn't enough, I was told part of the curriculum was what the school called "Drill" where all students would gather and practice an array of marching formations on a weekly basis. And if that wasn't enough, upon entering fifth grade, I would be able to march with a (prop) rifle. It all seemed surreal and felt like it would be a lot of fun.

Without question, McDonogh had many positive elements. But in terms of me, in retrospect, I found the negatives outweighed the positives. I was at McDonogh for eight years. Yes, the academic program was good. But, again, me being me at the time, so much of what went on in the classroom was lost. Over my head. Uninteresting. At the time, each grade was divided into three academic levels: "A" being for the highest achievers; "B" being for the second highest level; and "C" for those at the bottom of the rung. Every year I was part of the "C" grouping. Any individual seeking entrance into McDonogh was given some type of entrance exam. Upon stepping into the first grade, I am not sure how or why I was placed in that lowest tier. Did I not stay within the lines to satisfy the examiners? Was I not as handy with Lincoln logs as I should have been? Not sure. I remember receiving no explanation either from the school or my parents for how I was ranked. As the years there passed, I never did work my way out of that lower tier. Yes, there was a bit of a stigma attached to that. But mostly for myself, I never minded all that much. My thoughts as I would gaze out the classroom window were directed more on the activities occurring on the school's various athletic fields. It seemed a lot more appealing than whatever was being discussed in class.

This is not to say the classes were a complete bore. One day the calm of the class was interrupted when a student in the row next to mine let out a terrible yelp. It turned out he was playing with a stapler and accidently stapled his hand. He never made it out of the third tier either.

McDonogh was a combination boarding-commuter school. My

parents had the option of letting me live on campus but opted to have me commute each day. That was fine by me even though it made my school days very long. I would leave home shortly after seven in the morning and not return home till close to 5:30 p.m. A long day for anyone. Because we did not live all that close to the campus, I was always among the first to be picked up by the school bus and nearly the last to be dropped off each day. No time for walking, certainly during the week. Weekends proved to be the only time for that refuge. But with one or both of my parents home on Saturdays and Sundays, such an activity was not always possible or practical. At times, spending time in my room served as an adequate substitute for walking. Not ideal, but good-enough.

Did I envy my neighborhood friends who went to school very close to their homes? Not too much. The only time it bothered me was when all of us were together and they would begin talking about their shared experiences at school, teachers they had, etc. My experiences were not theirs. The cast of characters in my life were not ones they knew and vice versa. Consequently, they would talk and laugh about their adventures at school. I would listen and do little sharing because my stories were not ones involving anyone they knew. I was content to not be heard. Comfortable with rarely being asked to talk about school days with my friends. Much easier to ask the others about themselves. More than that, I sincerely enjoyed hearing those "others," including friends and family, talk about themselves. More interesting than what I might have to say. Interestingly, over the coming years that would not change. To speak up would be to draw attention; to be in the spotlight; to be assessed by others. Who would want that? Not me. Perhaps, also, those days were the beginning of a realization on my part that folks, generally, prefer to be heard rather than listen. Talk to more than talk with. In being quiet, I was giving them what they wanted while also subconsciously gathering information about those around me. Getting to know them so I could best address their interests, and even needs, and better connect with them when I did speak. I was consciously letting their focus sit in the front seat of my intellectual "car" while I moved mine to the back. I am saying that not so much to suggest I was on my way to being selfless. Rather, at least in those days, I was reinforcing my negative assessment of me. Others were more important than me. Besides, I could and would give me and my priorities the spotlight or, at least, equal time in my walks and time alone.

Where I did step happily into the spotlight was on the playing field.

My kind of classroom. My kind of "stage." Sports came easy to me. Studying did not. There was no homework with sports. Just put on gym shorts and I was good-to-go. Classes, on the other hand, required focus. Intellectual discipline. Taking tests. Speaking out in-class. Being assessed in a way I did not want. Class time was my quiet time. Only with reluctance did I ever speak out. There were even times when the teacher would call on me and I would not respond. Just sit there for fear of embarrassing myself. That fear was not unique to elementary school classes. Ironically, by not saying anything in response to a direct question from the teacher, I was embarrassing myself anyway. Perhaps more so. Such moments replayed in my mind even into my college years. Teachers, I discovered, are less forgiving in college than they are when students are younger than ten years of age. That whole spot-light-thing was just not my cup of tea right from the beginning. It is still not. Later, I became adept at avoiding being the center of attention. One big way was to direct questions toward others. Get them to share. They talk. I listen. I was helped along by the fact that I really did have a genuine interest in what others had to say. Listening, for me, actually was a source of enjoyment.

It was in the fifth grade that my vision began to fade. More and more during class I would need to rise from my seat and move toward the chalkboard in order to see what the teacher had written. Even then I had to squint. I finally said something to my parents about this. Result: trip to the eye doctor and glasses. I say this as one more example of my being less-than as hardly any of my friends or peers were wearing glasses. In the years that followed I came to accept this change but even now do not like it.

At best, my grades were average. Mostly below that. Still, good enough to pass. Nellie and Herman Walsch's son was not going to be a scholar. They would never be able to slap a bumper sticker on their car that said, "My son is an A student at…" Still, this is not to say I did not learn valuable lessons at McDonogh. It was 1959, the beginning of our fourth grade. On our way to school that morning our bus made an unfamiliar stop. Who should step on but a black person. First grader. It was not till later that I learned he was the first African American student in McDonogh's 86-year history. The boy's named was Milton and here he was on my bus. He seemed nervous and sat in a seat by himself. We all stared at him. No question he could feel our eyes. Sometime between then and when we arrived at school I rose from my seat and sat next to him. I had no agenda.

No topics of conversation to pursue. He just seemed alone and I thought some company could help. This was not the start of a deep and lasting friendship, however. Because he was in the first grade and I was in the fourth, our paths during the day did not cross. In fact, we were in separate buildings. But we did talk on the bus rides to and from school. I remember little else beyond that in terms of our interactions. Milton seemed like a nice enough guy. Not much time passed before he stopped looking as if he were alone.

One lesson I learned from him is that feelings of isolation while with others are not to be ignored. Stepping into a group or crowd of people without specific others with whom to connect is a lonely experience. My times alone, generally, were by choice. That is different. But seeing someone feeling isolated by circumstances rather than choice should not be something from which we turn away. That was young Milton's situation. I do not remember any of what we talked about or if we talked about much of anything in those early days. I do remember that in the coming days others sat with him, too, and that within weeks he was acting as silly as the rest of us while traveling to and from school. Communication in such circumstances is such a powerful tool. It does not necessarily have to be via word. Actions matter, too, I learned.

As a semi-military academy, McDonogh, not surprisingly, had rules. As students advanced from one grade to the next, those showing signs of leadership were given military ranks such as lieutenant or captain. (In my case, by the time I had completed the eighth grade, I had been elevated to the rank of corporal. The only fellow students this gave me authority over were the ones without rank.) No doubt a key reason for my lowly standing was the high number of demerits I had accumulated while there. Demerits could be assigned by higher-ranking students and, of course, teachers. They were given out if one was judged to be breaking any rules or misbehaving in some way. In this area, I distinguished myself. I accumulated so many demerits that several times I had to go out to campus on Saturdays to work them off. Among the work I and others had to do included raking leaves, picking up trash or spending the entire day in what was called "study hall." This was a big lecture hall where we had to sit and at least give the impression we were reading our textbooks and taking notes. But definitely no talking.

Funny. I do not remember me being a rebel or one to buck authority. Still, given my track record of low grades and constantly being disciplined, on some level I must have been inclined to resist authority, unfair or otherwise. Collectively, this must have added to the concerns my parents had that they had produced a child destined to travel the path of mediocrity. Of the two, my mother was better at hiding whatever concerns she did have. Dad, on the other hand, had a lousy poker face. His seeds of impatience with me were planted during those early years. I sensed his constant disappointment. I sensed his frustration at not being able to fix me. It made me constantly nervous around him. Perhaps a little afraid. On the flip side, I hated myself for not living up to my mother's high expectations of me. Yes, she saw bright lights and goodness in me. She was my champion. But the hard truth was I lacked the credentials or track record of success to support her vision of me. I just wish I had given her more to work with for her times when she would get together with her sisters and they would begin their periodic bragging sessions about their children. Contending with the ying and yang of my parents left me not so much in the middle of their dealings with me as it did off on the sidelines. Was I great or not? Was I a star or also-ran? I sensed I was falling short in both their eyes despite the opportunities they were placing before me. It was enough for me to take one long walk after another and throw myself into athletics as much as I could.

As my eighth grade year came to an end, my parents and I came to a mutual agreement that perhaps McDonogh was not the best fit for me. Though mom and dad said they would keep sending me there if I wanted to continue and the powers-that-be at the school said they would allow me to stay enrolled, the decision was reached that I should try my luck at public school. That was fine by me. To my way of thinking, I would no longer have to wear a military uniform and I could be closer to my neighborhood friends most every day. Like purchasing a lottery ticket. The change ultimately would be just what I needed to become all that I was expected to be—something, I should note, I had no clue would look like. Thus, I began my years in a co-ed environment for the first time as well as the final third of pre-college schooling.

Did that new "lottery ticket" pay off? Did I shine like never before? No. Still shy. Still an introvert. A few new friends but not a lot. Grades remained as they were before. Did I mention that I was in class with girls? That meant a lot of not-too subtle staring on my part. Not much beyond that, however. Girls aside, I was a new kid and with that came the challenge to distinguish myself in some way. Fit in. The school year was not very far along when I got into a shoving match with another kid on the school bus ride home. I no longer remember the whys and wherefores of it. I just knew I could not back down when he took a swing at me on the bus. The driver kicked us both off the bus. But instead of just me and the guy getting off, four of his friends got off, too. As the bus drove away, there I stood surrounded. Taunts followed. I knew enough to know that if I started swinging, the result would not be good for me. I walked away and did not look back. Embarrassed. Angry. Belittled. Grateful not to get beat up.

The next day the driver informed the principal's office of what happened. The result: I would have to find my own way to and from school. The next morning, mom began driving me to school. After school, I walked home. It stayed that way the remainder of the entire academic year. More disappointment from my parents. More disappointment in myself. More isolation. More walking. So, it was not a total set-back. Still, surely one of these days I would start doing well. Start getting things right. That day, obviously, had not arrived.

I could not wait to complete my time at that school despite the daily opportunity to travel by-foot and muse about most anything other than school. The next year I moved onto senior high school. The big time. Like entering the major leagues except not on the wings of merit. The result, I figured, may not be any better but at least the school was situated closer to our home so my commute would be easier for everyone. Fortunately, this moment in my evolution was better than the ones before it. I made more friends. And there were opportunities for me to play sports. Most surprisingly, I even began showing slight improvement in the area of grades. Nothing dramatic but a glimmer that there was life in my noggin beyond an array of baseball statistics.

In addition to the primary course subjects, the school offered electives. One was called "journalism." I decided to give it a try as I needed the credit and nothing else was of much interest to me. In the words of Robert Frost, it turned out to be a road that "made all the difference." This is not to say that suddenly I became an honors student. But I can report that I did raise my grades enough to the point where I could be classified as "average." Mostly grades of C mixed with too many Ds and an occasional B. Maybe not a giant leap for mankind, but certainly one for me.

I liked journalism. I liked observing others. I liked being the one who asked questions with little worry of being asked anything in return. This gave me a sense of control. Also, it gave me a degree of autonomy while at the same time an excuse for being involved, close to the action of my environment. I was able to collect information, gain knowledge, and gather insight. Being a reporter, I found, put me in a position of a certain kind of acceptance where it was acceptable for me to be close yet not say much. To maintain this position, the trick—actually there were several—was to get people to talk to me and then do a decent job of reporting their words and actions. The good news is I found that I was genuinely interested in what others had to share. My biggest challenge was two-fold: being able to come up with stimulating questions to trigger interest on the part of my subjects to give me good answers and turning myself into a halfway decent and accurate writer. On a more practical level, this journalism class gave me the idea that perhaps I could major in that field in college—at least until I figured out what I really wanted to do. Also, more and more, it was becoming my personal sweet spot in place of athletics. It was during this time when my ability to dominate others on the various ball fields and courts was beginning to seriously decline. In my case, such a reality was as unwanted as it was unstoppable.

Upon entering my senior year, like most everyone else, I began looking at college. Every college to which I applied had a good journalism program. Perhaps even more notable, they were all out-of-state. They represented a chance for me to branch-out, go out on my own. The prospect of that represented an acknowledgement that this was something I needed to do even if it did make me nervous. It was possible, I conceded, that moving away from one would not only make me feel further distance from others, but it would be another failed attempt at my doing something successfully. I shared my desire to attend an out-of-state college with my parents and, to my surprise, they agreed. Mom and dad said they were all right with my living away from home. Fortunately, they also had enough money in their bank accounts to afford it. Given my grade point average, I sure was not going to be awarded any scholarship money.

So, it was fall, 1968, when my parents drove me to Knoxville, Tennessee, to begin the next chapter in my educational journey and life. University of Tennessee. Journalism major. Get the degree. Use it to get a job. Make money. That seemed straight forward enough. Lots of others were doing it. Why not me? Tears filled my eyes as my parents drove away. What was I thinking? What was I doing here? What would have been so bad about going to a local college back home? What an idiot! The beginning days at college could not have been worse. I missed home. Heavy rain fell on the first day of class. Going from one class to another I slipped while trying to navigate a muddy embankment. I ended up bursting into that class with muddy shoes, pants, hands. Very embarrassing. When does the next bus out of town leave?

Friends I made largely revolved around guys I met in my dormitory or in class. I had no interest in trying to pledge or join a fraternity even though it was a big part of campus life. Becoming part of that scene did not strike me as something I wanted to be part of. Even then I was not much of a joiner. Still, every so often on weekend nights I would walk past several frat houses and hear lots of laughter and music and wonder what it would be like to be part of that. The university gave students living on campus opportunities to select their own roommates. I opted to hope-for-the-best. The majority of the people I roomed with were decent and friendly-enough, no one I did not get along with at least on the surface. Almost all of them were from Tennessee, so, unlike me, they already had people at the university that they knew. Sometimes I hung out with them and their friends and sometimes I kept to myself. When on my own, I made myself at home—lots of walking around campus and even in parts of Knoxville. More sights to take-in. More nooks and crannies that help give a city its personality. Record stores. Books stores. Even movie theaters. They became my go-to places.

Fast forward to the last half of my sophomore year. My grades were horrible. So, too, were my study habits. I found that no matter the level of enthusiasm one might have for reaching a specific goal, achieving it still requires the work ethic to roll up one's sleeves and do the work and do it well. One would have thought I learned that lesson while in middle or high school. No. Consequently, I was on the verge of being dismissed from the university. Flunking out. At this point, I was the only one who knew this. My parents were not notified as it was the university's protocol to communicate directly with the student.

What to do? Mom and dad would be mortified. Me, too. This reality had to be faced. I had to talk to someone. Do something to make this not happen. I finally decided to sit down with my faculty advisor, a professor within the university's department of communication. He was also one of my instructors. We looked at my transcript—the good, bad and ugly of it—and calculated that if a grade in any one of my classes could be raised by single letter, then my overall academic status would be elevated from dismissal to academic probation. We went over all the communication classes up to that point that I had taken. It turned out the most logical one where the final grade could be raised was in one that I had taken under him, my advisor. After a few seconds of coming to this realization, we looked up at each other. He finally said there was no way he would do that without reasonable justification. He instructed me to leave. Give it serious thought, he said, and come back to see him by day's end the next day if I had anything he could work with. This is what I did. More walking. More thinking. More hand-wringing. Finally, an idea.

The Professor seemed surprised when he looked up from his desk the next day to see me at his office door. I pitched my idea. During my freshman year at UT, I had written a lengthy profile of one of the members of the school's football team for the university's yearbook. It had been well received by the player, the team, and the university community. I asked my professor if he would use this as an extra credit assignment to justify raising my grade by a single letter. For me, the proposal could only be described as a Hail Mary pass. Fortunately, the professor was familiar with the piece. He said he would think about it that evening. Come see him the next day. I did. Without any dramatic pause he said he would make the grade-change but emphasized that I had to get my academic act together. If not, then I would be gone and he would be there to hold the door for me to expedite my departure. Fair enough. Two years later as I was preparing to graduate from UT, I went to see the professor to thank him for his great kindness. He professed not to remember what I was talking about. True or not, I sure remembered. Still do obviously. I needed a hand at a self-inflicted dicey time in my life and he gave it to me.

The university adjusted my academic status giving me another academic year to raise my grade point average. It would be so nice to say I was like Rocky Balboa, rose from the canvas and knocked out Apollo Creed; that is, earned a 4.0 G.P.A. the next semester. I did not. But my overall grades were good enough to raise my G.P.A. a few percentage points. The same thing happened the next semester. And the semester after that. Maybe graduating with a bachelor's degree in communication was in the cards after all.

I never shared any of this with my parents. Nor with any of my friends or family members. They never knew how close I came to flunking out of college. Even now, I shudder at how close I came. What would have happened if I had been dismissed? What path would I have taken then? Probably college near home. Or maybe not. Occasionally, that "What if?" game pops up in my head. After all this time, I remain uncertain. Thankfully, I never had to find out.

Shortly after this close call with the university's academic standards folks, I took a big step outside my comfort zone. Up till then, I had lived in the biggest dormitory on campus—Hess Hall—which was also one of the largest in the entire Southeast Conference of universities. Nearly twelve hundred male and female students lived there. At the beginning of each academic year the dorm had student elections for dorm officers to represent the entire population before the student housing office and other pertinent administrative units. I ran for president and won. My one and only foray into politics. I remember very well enjoying the extra responsibilities that came with this position as well as the opportunity to work with an array of people on campus. That aside, I can see clearly now how taking on this extra work on the heels of my barely escaping being dismissed from the university was not the smartest of moves. Given what had almost happened, I should have put all my energies into my studies. No, not me. Zigging when I should have been zagging. I do not precisely recall what motivated me to pursue this elected office, but in a more general way, I do know the lure of stepping into a position of visible responsibility having a strong appeal. But the notion of stepping forward and having others openly assess me was not an easy one to face. I liked the prospect of fellow students saying "Yes, he's my guy." However, the reality that there would be others—possibly more—who would take the opposite view would be a tough pill to swallow. As luck would have it, those folks turned out to be in the minority. Still, had I been thinking more clearly, I would not have run for this office. Yet I did and it worked out. Another "Whew" moment in my life.

Did this role put me in a position of power? No. But what it did give me was access, not just to administrators within the university's housing office but also to fellow students who lived in the dormitories. Yes, I now had a voice which was given attention, but more than that, I had a more profound opportunity to use my ears. This was perhaps the best part of that experience. It gave me greater experience in listening only in a more meaningful way. Representing others, I was in a position to hear directly about the concerns of other students as they related to living away from home and interacting with people representing various ethnic and religious backgrounds and then help address their concerns beyond just saying, "I hear you." Being student president of the largest dormitory on campus provided me with an opportunity to step outside myself and in doing so be able to help others—even in a small way. I liked it. Very much. In terms of tangible contributions, one focus of mine was attempting to deflate racial tension between white and black students. I was able to help ease those problems by initiating open dialogues between the students as well as by bringing in outside experts on matters of race. This was a major source of pride for me even as I struggled with my own academic challenges.

When I entered the University of Tennessee in fall, 1968, I wanted to complete my degree in four years, figuring that is the timeline most everyone would be following. But as I approached what normally would have been my final semester there, I realized upon its completion I would still be twenty-four credit hours short. That is the equivalent of eight, three-credit classes. As I could not change the fact that I would not be graduating at the conclusion of the spring semester, my new goal was to come as close as I possibly could to doing that. By my thinking, that meant that I had to take all eight classes during the coming summer terms; a giant load under most any circumstances as each class was approximately four weeks in duration. The workload for each would be heavy and intense and unrelenting. Still, if I were to graduate around the time of my friends, it would help ensure no one would be the wiser as to how close I had come to flunking out. I had to go for it. My driving goal was to avoid any risk of embarrassment with family and friends back home. Oh, and there was also the matter of earning a college degree.

I did it. Not totally sure how other than good old-fashioned buckling down. Granted, I maintained my streak of not earning any As. But a passing grade is a passing grade is a passing grade. I even managed to raise my final grade point average to C. Nothing to brag about, but good enough to pass and earn an undergraduate degree in journalism. My final day at UT revolved around one last final exam. I walked into the classroom building with my car packed and parked just outside the main entrance. Two hours later I walked out of the building, hopped into the car and drove away. That was it. It felt good, of course, but as I put the campus in my rearview mirror part of me was feeling that I was making a narrow escape rather than completing a college experience. The fact is I did not distinguish myself there. My parents sensed it and I knew it. They did ask, but with little conviction, if I wanted to participate in the university's graduation ceremony. My response was an emphatic "no." As a student, I had underperformed. I did not earn the celebration that often comes with a graduation ceremony. At the same time, for the first time, an odd feeling that I was better than my academic record to-date indicated began stirring within me. In retrospect, more than anything, that feeling was UT's great gift to me: realizing the possibility that I was better than I had thus far shown myself to be.

Over forty-five years would pass before I returned for a quick visit to the UT-Knoxville campus one weekend afternoon while traveling with my wife, Jo, from Virginia to Texas. She was curious to see it. Me, too. Stepping back onto campus, I was not overwhelmed with emotion or hardly any wave of nostalgia. What did and still does stick with me is how lucky I was to graduate from there at all; and how blessed I was that a single professor showed me compassion.

Slightly over four years later—1976—I began to get an itch to try my hand at more schooling. By now, I was working at a community college in Maryland. I enjoyed it. I enjoyed the atmosphere of an institution of higher learning. I figured if I was going to turn that satisfaction into a full-time arrangement and perhaps rise in the administrative hierarchy, then a graduate degree would be worth considering. Even more than that, it would be necessary. That year, I enrolled at what was then called Bowie State College in Maryland and began working toward a master's degree in education administration. Three years later that degree was done. Three years after that, I began working toward a second master's degree—this one in communication—at Towson University, also in Maryland. My thinking was it would complement the earlier graduate degree. Plus, it would strengthen my professional credentials should opportunities for job promotion arise. It took me three years to make that degree mine as well.

I attended the graduation ceremonies at both of those institutions. My parents did, too. My academic effort at Bowie State and Towson was much more to my liking. No way was I ever the best budding scholar to grace either campus, but I sure was not the worst. At those times in my life, given where I had been, that reality was good enough. These back-to-back achievements made me proud in a quiet yet deep and lasting way. My evolution from being in that C section at McDonogh School to having earned two master's degrees injected a level of intellectual confidence into my psyche that I had not previously known. While I still saw myself as that struggling undergraduate student who narrowly escaped academic dismissal, the two degrees led me to begin altering my self-image—like moving pieces of furniture in a room to allow for more sunlight to shine in. Still, even now, I have not allowed myself to forget my poor academic performances of the past any more than my sharp decline in athletics. The spotlight has a way of disappearing with alarming and uncompromising speed unless one continues to commit themselves to working hard and respecting the challenges before them.

My book-learning was not over yet. Since the second master's degree the possibility of earning a doctorate began bouncing around in head. But could I do it? Did I have the time and energy and intellectual chops? What about the work ethic? I was not sure. Years passed. I was in my mid-50s. My hair began turning gray and the bounce in my step began to lessen. Even my time to go walking decreased. Plus, my career growth was leveling off, so the prospect of earning a doctorate and benefitting from it with a promotion or hefty pay hike was, at best, slight. If I was going to go for it and actually obtain this degree, then it would have to be for me. Only me. A private achievement in a public setting. The satisfaction of crossing that finish line would have to be reward enough.

There was also the matter of my own deep-rooted insecurities to consider. Going as far back as my time at McDonogh School, I had fantasized about others viewing me as smart. I had my doubts. In all fairness, I had certainly given myself reason to believe my self-doubt was justified. Throughout my adult years I had done my best to hide those insecurities. Not let anyone know that within me were feelings of being second-rate when it came to matters of the mind. While a doctorate would not necessarily erase those feelings, this degree would go a long way toward influencing others to view me either as a smart cookie or one that was at least borderline shrewd or intellectually sound; a person when speaking seriously was worth listening to; a person whose intellect was worthy of respect. Just as important, my negative learning assessment of me, at that point, might not carry as much weight as it had.

Why was this so damn important? Why did this matter of my perceived intelligence carry so much weight within me? Was there a mystical club that I wanted to be part of that only so-called smart people could join? Did achieving the highest academic degree that could be conferred represent a level of acceptance in and by me that up till now I had not been able to achieve? I longed to be proud of me. In some ways I was. Yet the level of self-respect to which I longed continued to remain beyond my reach—in sight but not quite within my grasp. Was a doctorate the missing piece that would fill whatever holes within my psyche that existed? Probably not entirely but maybe. Without question, it would be a significant step in the right direction. As one who had spent a lifetime contending with those feelings, this was a gap that hurt. It needed to be filled. It is a hurt I never shared with anyone. I kept it hidden with jokes and self-deprecating comments about my intelligence that were more spot-on than many realized. "You are so modest," many would say. Little did they know that I was being unsparingly honest. Little did they know that I was on a non-stop quest to seek out opportunities that would enable me to nullify failures or missed opportunities from the past. In my heart—most of it anyway—I knew I could do better than I did at McDonogh School or Woodlawn Middle School or Woodlawn Senior High School or the University of Tennessee. Earning a doctorate represented a major opportunity at my own redemption, a chance to strike an important balance between my overall record of growth and self-worth as a person. This was the real reason why I wanted and, yes, needed to go for this degree. It would be for me. I was not so much interested in whatever cheers or accolades would come from others. It was my own cheer that I wanted and needed to hear the most.

The year was 2008, twenty-nine years after earning that second master's degree. As luck would have it, George Mason University, situated in Northern Virginia, an institution I had joined in January, 1989, was introducing a doctorate program in communication. Naturally, it was to be housed in the university's communication department. I had been teaching part-time in that department for several years, so I knew the faculty administrators there and they knew me. Maybe—just maybe—they would accept me as among the program's first wave of doctoral students. They did. It turned out the first class of entries in the program numbered a whopping three. Later, I joked that I was among the top three in my class. At this point, I was nearly sixty years of age. "The old guy" easily by three decades in the program's numerous classes. The three of us found ourselves surrounded by master's level students. We were all taking the same classes. The difference is we were required to do more work. Fair enough. I found being surrounded by youth with their energy and enthusiasm was not a bad way to go. But it was also intimidating, at least for me. My fellow students seemed to be a lot more on top of their game than me. Much more computer savvy. There was also the matter of my overall schedule: husband, full-time job, teaching part-time, and now working toward a doctorate. Overload anyone? But as has been said, the heart wants what the heart wants. Whatever time management skills I had were about to be tested to the fullest. I jumped in with no life jacket. My opportunity to fulfill a dream. No expectations beyond that.

Time passed and approximately three years later I had completed the program's required course work. Reports. Reading assignments. Class presentations. Research papers. Group projects. Given my schedule, I had little time for massaging my schoolwork. Everything I did had to be "good enough" on the first go-around. Nothing halfway or mediocre. Acceptable to my instructors. Worthy of a passing grade. Work that I could feel good about and that would bring credit to the program—even with the passage of time. This effort was not unlike my final summer semester at the University of Tennessee when I earned twenty-four credits over a twelve-week period. Buckle down. Give everything my best shot and hope it was acceptable.

It was now time for the final hurdles: two comprehensive exams and the dissertation. First, the written and oral comps. Approaching them, the department gave a huge helping hand. They gave me and the other doctoral students the topics around which the questions would revolve. "This is awesome," I thought. I interpreted their assistance as making whatever studying I was going to do a great deal easier. It was a most foolish assumption, one that almost sabotaged my chances of successfully completing the program. I failed to realize that by giving us a heads-up on the exam topics the department was communicating that, in return, it expected our answers to be very thorough, well thought-out, and strong. The other students picked up on this. I did not. They saw it as an opportunity to demonstrate their worthiness as being fully accepted by the university and academia in-general as serious scholars. I saw it as a formality. A short-cut. My two colleagues were wise. I was not. They were respectful. I was arrogant.

The first part of the comprehensive exam was the written section. Yes, I studied but not all that hard. I took the test and walked away thinking my responses were acceptable. They weren't. My faculty adviser sat me down and said several of my responses were, in fact, deemed so incomplete that the graders of the test wanted me to re-take them. I did but quickly learned that my do-over was not all that much better than my original effort. This left the faculty members who were assessing my fate in a quandary: give me a failing grade or allow me to move forward to the oral part of the exam with the hope I would do well enough on it to earn an overall passing grade.

They decided, reluctantly I learned later, to let me proceed to the oral exam. It would be a three-hour grilling on issues relating to communication, including the topics I failed to properly address on the written exam. My faculty advisor warned me that as a result of my sub-par performance on the written exam, the oral exam would be especially challenging. As this was a new program, the faculty did not want to give anyone the impression that their standards were easy or lower than any of the other more-established doctoral programs offered at the university. They had something to prove. I did, too.

By nature, I am not a confident person. I am not one to step into a ring with my sleeves rolled up, telling those around me, "I got this." I wish I were. In-truth, sometimes I wish there were two of me, so that there was enough of me to carry around all my self-doubt. Often, it seems, one of me is not enough for that. Approaching this oral exam, my self-doubts were working over-time. A week away from it and I still was not sure how best to prepare. Memorize every communication theory that I could think of? Fat chance. My options were limited. With the set date—a Friday morning—rapidly approaching, it seemed I had to go old-school and do my best to become as familiar with the theories and historical figures, sweeping trends in the field, and overall information as best I could. Treat this gathering as a book club where folks gather to have an enlightened discussion on the topic at-hand. Think of this more as a conversation than a cross-examination. At the same time, embrace the possibility of falling short and accepting that win or lose, I was going to be okay. Those around me would be fine. My life and theirs would carry on. This self-talk was designed to ease the pressure I was feeling. It helped. What also helped was the guidance of my wife, Jo. She proved to be an ideal study-buddy. She kept me focused. She kept me engaged. She made sure I did not stop believing in myself. And she helped make sure that I did not give this challenge any more power than it deserved.

To this day, I credit her even more than myself for passing the oral exam. Just before stepping into that room where the four faculty members sat, I took a deep break and told myself for one of the few times in my life, "I got this." For that moment, I came as close as ever to actually meaning it. Pleasantries were exchanged. Small-talk was kept to a minimum. Me and them. My inquisitors were challenging, in my face, every so often differential, always respectful, relenting, and, ultimately, satisfied with their challenges and convinced I had responded to them with all I had. At the conclusion of our interaction, they asked me to step outside the room so they could discuss my performance. Though I did not know what they would say, I felt okay. I had done my best. Done as well as I could. Whatever happened after that would be all right. What did happen after that was more than all right. I passed. Handshakes all around. If I knew how to do a proper backflip, I would have done it. I called my wife. Her whoop was all the backflip I needed.

One more hurdle. The dissertation. A challenge by any standard. But one much more within my wheelhouse. It involved writing and talking with people. This was a challenge I felt much more confident I could do, do well, and defend successfully. My faculty advisor told me it would probably take me well over a year to complete this task, possibly even two. At this point, a new semester was about to begin. Five months long. I told her that I was going to do what needed to be done within that time span. She rolled her eyes and said, "We'll see." Her understandable reservations, coupled with my determination, was all the incentive I needed. I did not want this to drag on, nor did I want to get bogged down in the back-and-forth that inevitably characterizes all-but-dissertation (ABD) students and members of their dissertation committee. I had a clear vision of what I wanted my paper to address and what needed to be done to make it coherent and complete as it needed to be. I set precise weekly goals for myself and my committee members when they needed to be brought-in to my efforts. This train of mine, I had decided, was going to do more than run on-time. It would be ahead of schedule.

Five months later I walked across the stage at the university's commencement to receive my diploma. The President of the university gave me a hug that I will long remember. He also gave me my diploma. I will remember that, too. I was now Doctor Daniel Walsch. The trek from years in the bottom tier of students at McDonogh School to earning a high school diploma, an undergraduate degree, two master's degrees, and, finally, a PhD was an amazing ride. A humbling journey as well. It lasted forty-three years. I benefitted greatly from the good will of others. Perhaps they saw signs of potential in me that I did not recognize. Perhaps they were just being kind. Perhaps both. Either way, they could have turned away my requests for help. Such a choice would have been justified and understandable. Instead, those teachers and many fellow students held a door for me when I was not even sure where the handle was. Their actions continue to inspire choices I make when I deal with others, including students. How many times should one be given an opportunity to succeed, to be given a chance to rise, take another swing at the ball, speak up for themselves? I am forever grateful that, in my case, people in my academic travels had it within them to choose in my favor. With another nod to Robert Frost, thanks to those others, that road that they enabled me to travel made "all the difference."

My dissertation was titled, "A Strategic Communication to a Crisis Communication Situation." It was a comparative analysis of unique situations that occurred at George Mason University and Northern Illinois University. At George Mason, it was the great success of its men's basketball team making it to the coveted Final Four circle in the annual NCAA basketball tournament. At Northern Illinois, the situation was the killing of multiple students by a lone gunman. In my paper, I contended that both incidents represented examples of crisis communication. Several months after successfully completing and defending my dissertation, I was contacted by Lambert Academic Publishing in Germany about the possibility of publishing it as a book. I jumped at their surprise offer. As a result, 2011 became the year I not only earned a doctorate, but also became a published author. The "Acknowledgements" section of the book reads, in part, "…I also wish to express great thanks to the numerous professors who were so generous to me with their wisdom and expertise in the classes I took with them. Each of these scholars did so much to help me keep my head above water throughout my entire doctoral program. And the same holds true for so many of my fellow students. You are the greatest. Finally, but far from the least, I give thanks to my wife, Jo. Simply put, she is my best friend, my life's companion and my North Star."

I only wish my parents had been around to see this turn-of-events. No way would they have seen this coming. Truth-be-told, I did not either for the longest time even though I sure wanted it. While in their hearts, they may not have always believed in my abilities, they never stopped doing all they could to make sure I had as many opportunities as I needed to achieve whatever goals I set for myself.

5

The Professional Me

Biologist and naturalist E.O. Wilson once talked of humans existing within what he described as a fixed order of life stages. The key challenge people face, he observed, is figuring out where to go that takes them beyond their own biological boundaries. Wilson mused, "The world can at least hope for a stable ecosystem and a well-nourished population. But what then?" Indeed. So much of my early life was spent trying to decide where it is I wanted to go. Of course, I had my walks with specific destinations. But now, what were my destinations beyond the walks? Yes, I was still doing a great deal of walking but little of it was spent moving toward something other than my own head-talk. While time to reflect is important, by itself the prospect of it adding to one's ability to contribute to mankind is small or, more to the point, finding and maintaining a substantiative meaning that requires purpose. The less time one spends not knowing where they are headed, the more time they have available to become fulfilled or, on a larger scale, become a genuinely contributing member of society or the overall human race. In *Alice in Wonderland*, Lewis Carroll noted that if one does not know where they are going, then any road will take them there. How right he was. People need some type of compass, be it in the form of a profession or calling to where they can better contribute to the welfare of themselves or others. Such a sense of direction is vital to a substantial life. In my case, other than my foggy fantasy of becoming a professional baseball player, I did not go through high school or even much of my time in college with a firm notion of what I wanted to do or where I wanted to go.

A clarity of purpose, for me, did not suddenly reveal itself in one notable moment. At best, it crept up on me. Walking remained an emotional and physical "fix." But more and more this act cried out for an intellectual companion on which I could focus, wrestle with, embrace, etc. beyond simply distancing myself from my current uncertainty. My walks, though enjoyable, needed greater intellectual substance than I had been giving them. This, at least, represented a sense that I was slowly beginning to recognize a need to shift my intellectual focus on matters of what I viewed as substance or weight. In my walks, I thus began to include reflections on how best to step into adulthood. For me, it meant embracing the reality that I was no longer a child. The time had come that I had to stop thinking like one. Even though I had yet to define exactly what it meant for me to adequately reflect on myself and the world more like a grown-up, I sensed the time had arrived for me to begin seeing myself and the world in that context in a more direct and meaningful way. My time of what I came to call "reactive drift" was coming to an end. What was to be its replacement was yet to come into focus.

This leads me to the field and act of communication. Many have put forth the notion that our first act as living beings is to breath; gasp for air. No question that makes sense. In my assessment of that, however, I have come to add an amendment. Tied for first as our initial act of living is one of communication. As a new-born, when we cry out for all to hear we are also communicating that we are alive, our journey out of our mother's womb has been successful. Mission accomplished, as it were. From that moment forward, everything we do is an act of communication. This continues right up to our final act of ceasing to breath. When that happens, we are also letting it be known that we are no longer alive. Breathing and communicating. The two are forever linked throughout all the variations of steps, actions, efforts, etc. we take between our birth and death. One does not occur without the other.

It has taken me decades to embrace this realization, to view the field and act of communication as the core of a person's existence. All that we study and do, whether it is the arts, science, math, technology, auto mechanics, mowing grass, athletics, etc. emanates from breathing and communicating much as warmth comes from a fire. Looking back, in my youth, long before I came even close to appreciating this—to me—truism or understanding it or being able to articulate it, I sensed the core power of communicating; the fundamental position it maintains in our daily existence. In my early years, perhaps this is what attracted me to the field of communication without my even realizing it. Journalism. Public relations. Doing it. Teaching it. Struggling with each. Becoming at least somewhat proficient in each. Continuing to seek ways to improve my ability to connect with others via the spoken word, written word and, above all, active listening.

Communication is more than simply identifying ways to be better heard, understood, or appreciated. It is more than coming up with strategies to influence the beliefs and actions of others. At its best, it is about making and maintaining connections and building on what folks have in-common and/or share. It epitomizes the idea that working toward one's self interest, ideally, should be done in the context of melding that preference with what is compatible with, if not best, for others. How realistic that is I will leave to others to determine. I concede achieving such an end is not easy as it means putting another's perspectives and/or wishes on a par with one's own. After all, is it not conventional wisdom for one to push ahead with what they want? To that I say, "yes and no." "Yes," we want what we want; but to deny that such singlemindedness does not affect or impact others in a potentially negative way is to deny reality. Consequently, the "no" part of my answer is that it makes more sense to act, including communicate, in a way that is more inclusive. Bottom line, I will always shout out as loudly as I can that this is a goal worthy of effort. As a professional, that is what I attempted with each effort at outreach: putting forth my message in the context of the perspectives and interests of others. Mindfulness. Personally, how close I come to that goal is how I measure whether my communicating attempts are successful. Even now, such a goal—regardless of how ideal or unrealistic it might be or seem—increases in importance to me with each passing day. To return to what my father once observed, in life we are an "us" a lot more than a "me." The challenge is to strike and maintain a healthy balance between fulfilling the two roles.

My first tangible step toward stepping into the world of communication began in high school. I enrolled in a journalism class as it seemed like a fairly painless elective to take. As part of that, I began writing for the school newspaper primarily for something to do. Even from my first article—whatever that was—I liked it. I found myself enjoying the act of journalism more and more, never mind the quality of my initial effort. As time passed, I even felt I was beginning to be halfway decent at working as a reporter. Still, even after being accepted into college as a journalism major, I was not

THE PROFESSIONAL ME

totally sold on the notion of working as a reporter for a living or career. This is despite the fact I would often tell others that this is what I wanted to do. It was a career decision that I talked myself into as I navigated my way through college. Some people, growing up, claim to know what they wanted to do since their early childhood. Not me. I eventually grew into my professional field: communication. I gradually came to embrace it like an old sweater that becomes more comfortable with each wearing.

I had worked at my college newspaper since my freshman year. News stories. Feature stories. An occasional editorial or column. Rarely did I turn down any assignment even if it meant having to skip a class or two. I believed I was contributing to the overall standing of the university itself. Besides, getting to interview the university president and VIPs that would come to campus or nearby was heady stuff. My first celebrity interview was with Duke Ellington. Bob Hope and Muhammed Ali were others. No doubt the encounter was as forgettable to them as it was unforgettable to me. Another time I went to see one of my communication professors as I had a brilliant idea for a story. I wanted to get his feedback before moving forward on it. Rumors had been circulating that officers within the City of Knoxville police department were abusing their prisoners. My idea was to get arrested so I could spend several nights in jail and then write a first-hand account of what I witnessed. I pitched my idea. The professor gave me a hard look and finally said, "So, let me get this straight. You want to have a criminal arrest on your permanent record so you can pursue a story you don't even know to be true?" It did not take me long to recognize that my brainstorm was more like a brain fart. I thanked him and quickly left his office. I shudder to think what would have happened had I proceeded without talking to anyone first. God only knows what crime I would have committed to get arrested.

Approaching the conclusion of my time at the University of Tennessee, I began the quest of all soon-to-be graduates-from-college: search for a job. Fortunately, I was able to secure several job interviews before graduating. Of those, the *Clarksville Leaf-Chronicle*, a mid-size newspaper situated about forty miles north of Nashville, made an offer to begin working for them in early fall. I would be a general assignment reporter. While I had wanted to return to Maryland, I also wanted to work and begin moving forward on what I hoped would be a respectful and successful career as a journalist. Approximately six months into the job, the top editor of the paper dangled an appealing carrot in front of me: my own weekly column in which I could write about the community, its residents and their day-to-day challenges. I loved that prospect. We agreed that we would begin moving forward on this "soon." Time passed but still no column. Instead, more news stories by me primarily on the city and county councils and police department. All interesting enough but a diversion from what I thought was going to be a sure thing: my own column. More time passed. Still no column. Encouraging hints from my boss but little more than that. Finally, he and I talked about my future. It turned out his initial mention of a column was, he said, him "thinking out loud." I was disappointed but not crushed or angry. Realistically, I was not sure if it was ever going to happen though I had high hopes. Besides, whatever insights into the community I had were still being formed. Plus, my writing was not strong enough at that point. More work was needed. More growth. Additionally, my writing "voice" was not nearly as distinct as I needed it to be. And I was still eager to return to Maryland. That meant updating my resume and searching for job possibilities in my home state.

My next newspaper was the *Hagerstown Morning Herald,* situated in Western Maryland. Much like Clarksville, nice community, decent work environment. I was hired as a general assignment reporter there, too. On my first day on the job, the editor picked up on the office police scanner that there was a major fire at a local apartment complex. My first assignment. A big story. Tragic one, too. One of the fatalities was a former employer at my new newspaper. More than that, it was the exact person whose place I had been hired to take. She was well-liked and respected both in the newsroom and by people who she covered as a reporter.

One of the major challenges for any reporter is to be a good listener. If you plan to quote people directly, it is vital you listen well enough to their words and understand the specific meaning of what it is they are trying to say. This is true even if you record their conversations or interviews. Context is vital to fully understanding the words that people put forth. As a young journalist, this was a challenge for me. Words, of course, are a key along with context and meaning—a truism I had yet to fully appreciate. Lacking a full appreciation of all that can lead to unfortunate misquoting or misrepresentation of issues and people. This was an issue for me in several stories that I worked on during my early months both in Tennessee and Maryland. On a few occasions, people claimed that I had misquoted them, not because I had invented statements they never made. Rather, they claimed to be taken out of context or not meaning what their specific words implied. At the time, I found their charges to be quite upsetting as I prided myself on being as accurate as possible in my reporting. At the same time, part of me believed those folks had a valid point. This drove me to focus even more intently on their statements by placing myself in their shoes as they answered my questions. In other words, I tried to become an even more active listener.

In my time at the *Morning Herald,* I covered several sensitive stories. One involved the suicide of the county sheriff, an act that caught his colleagues completely off-guard. When that happened, the city and county police departments had been my primary beat for several months. As a result, I had gotten to know many of the officers very well. I had gained their trust and, as a result, was given a great deal of access to them. Consequently, I was the only member of the press allowed inside the police station the day the news broke. While proud of that and my coverage, I found the experience quite upsetting. It resurrected memories of my high school friend.

Another stressful experience involved the Mack Truck company that had a branch operating in the geographic area of Washington County, Maryland, where my newspaper was located. Following interviews with Mack officials, I reported the company was going to close-down its operation in our area and relocate. Though quoted accurately, my primary source claimed this is not what he meant to say. The story generated a great deal of attention. It turned out Mack had no plans to relocate and that my main source—a top administrator—was in error when he shared this information with me. Even though he was disciplined by his superiors for his part in the inaccurate story, I found the whole episode to be quite stressful. My credibility was also challenged. Between that and the earlier story involving the sheriff, the experiences reminded me of the famous quote buy President Harry Truman: "If you can't stand the heat, then get out of the kitchen." My inclination was to get out of the kitchen. And that is what I did.

I began searching for a new job. This time, however, it would be different. I no longer wanted to continue working as a journalist. I wanted a job in a field that I considered having less built-in stress or tension. Fairly or not, journalists are viewed by many as adversaries. People to be avoided. I did not like that. I did not like the anxiety that came with constantly having to prove and/or defend one's intentions or integrity. But what were my alternatives? What profession could I pursue where I was able to utilize whatever skills I had developed up to that point as well as be viewed more as a team player rather than an enemy? While wrestling with those questions, I happened to be working with the public relations officer at a local community college on a series of stories at that institution. As we worked together, I found her duties to be of growing interest. They included collecting information, speaking on behalf of her college, and devising ways to best connect with the general public. Sliding over from my seat as a journalist to one as a public relations officer might be the best path for me to follow. With that in mind, I once again dipped my toe in the job market to see what opportunities there were for a guy like me—undergraduate degree, over three years professional experience in newspapers—looking to make a switch all under the umbrella of communication. Months passed with no luck. A few complimentary replies to my applications, but even under the most pleasant of situations, rejection is rejection. It hurts. It also added to my frustration at being in a job that I no longer wanted. Finally, summer of 1976, an invitation to come in for an interview came my way. It was from Anne Arundel Community College, located a few miles north of Annapolis.

My interview went as well as any I have ever had—before or since. My prospective boss, who had previously taught several foreign languages at the U.S. Naval Academy in Annapolis, was an older gentleman but very kind and supportive as he assessed my background and responded to the answers I gave to his questions. As his background was primarily in foreign languages, he did not have any direct experience in public relations either. We made a positive connection. After an hour or so in conversation, he offered me a job as his assistant director. I was thrilled and said, "Yes!" It was a very happy moment. After grins all-around, he raised the matter of salary. After receiving the job offer, that matter had temporarily slipped my mind. "Now there is a matter of what we can afford to pay you right now. This, after all, is a new position," he said.

He wrote the annual salary on a slip of paper and handed it to me. My salary would be forty-eight hundred dollars per year. Gulp. While I was not expecting to be given the keys to the kingdom, this sum was far lower than I had expected it would be. It was also lower than either one of my newspaper salaries. Though not having much experience in job interview situations, I knew enough to ask for a few days before making a final decision. I went home to begin some serious soul-searching with my then wife, Ida. The pros: a new job with new opportunities in a new field. Cons: relocating and trying to make financial ends meet on forty-eight hundred dollars per year without a guarantee as to when or by how much that would change.

After several rounds of back-and-forth, we decided to accept the offer and go from there all the while hoping for the best. The thinking was this kind of financial sacrifice was needed in order to get in the door of working in the field of public relations. Taking this step would eventually pay off, we reasoned with all fingers crossed. So, riding very much on both a wing and prayer, I entered the worlds of public relations and higher education. For the remainder of my years as a professional, I never looked back, nor did I ever completely leave either one.

I worked at Anne Arundel Community College for six years. During that time, I joined the Public Relations Society of America and even applied to gain professional accreditation as a public relations practitioner. The process involved taking a test and was an experience that proved far better than what I later struggled through in earning a doctorate. It was also successful. I could now put APR (accredited public relations) behind my name. In addition, I stepped into another world: teaching. Under the college's continuing education department, as a way of making a few extra dollars, I taught communication for several semesters at a nearby men's prison. A little scary? Yes. A bit intimidating. Yes. Intellectually rewarding? Without a doubt. Make no mistake, the first time I set foot in that environment with the doors locked behind me and no protection from any guards, I was ready to turn around and claim this had all been a gross misunderstanding. But I didn't. The classes were held in the men's recreation area under the watchful eyes of guards. They were not in the room with me but viewed what I and other instructors like me were doing through glass walls. Still, I was assured, they were prepared to take immediate action should the need arise much like lifeguards at a swimming pool.

Going into that class, prison officials warned me that an inmate might ask if he could reach out to me outside class via emails and telephone calls. I was told to decline any such request. As it turned out, several did attempt to open up communication channels with me. I was prepared and followed the advice of the experts. That aside, much to my surprise and relief, I found the inmates to be quite polite, seemingly interested in the information and insights I tried to share with them, and even respectful of what authority I had. I appreciated that as much as anything. Beyond the setting of my initial foray into teaching, this experience gave me a powerful taste of life in a classroom as the one yapping in front of the room rather than sitting behind a desk either taking notes or trying to stay awake. I liked it very much.

Teaching was counter to my introverted nature. Emotionally, that made it a struggle. The prospect of standing in front of a room of ranging from five or six students to over fifty represented a giant step outside my comfort zone. Yet given the constraints of a traditional class, including working with a specified time limit, I concluded that I would be in control of the agenda. I could work with that. Perhaps, in time, easily. Who knows? If I prepared well enough, I figured I just might be able to pull this "teaching-thing" off. Perhaps even make a connection with budding scholars on their way toward their own academic and professional goals. No question, though, teaching ran counter to my preference to avoid being the center of attention, preferring to stay within myself. It is a profession that carries with it an air of nobility and significance, particularly if done well. A job where one can inspire others to grow and move forward. The opportunity to be part of that outweighed my own nature; at least served as my justification for doing something I found fundamentally uncomfortable.

My stint at the men's prison did not last long. Nevertheless, I had been bitten by the teaching bug. To me, the question had quickly evolved from wondering whether I would ever do it again to begin seeking out my next opportunity. Nearly ten years would pass before that happened. Still, I was ready when that chance did arrive. It happened at Towson University, located just north of Baltimore. By then, I was working in the institution's university relations office. Towson University's department of communication needed a part-time instructor. I stepped forward and they invited me in.

Speaking of seeking ways to make extra money during this time, another on-the-side job I took was working as manager of a local movie theater. I mention it only because it was so damn fun. As I have always had a weak spot for movies, working at a theater was a real kick. This one had three screens. The young men and women I supervised were great and fun. Being able to eat all the popcorn I wanted—no cost—was like being given free-reign inside Willie Wonka's chocolate factory. Plus, there were the movies. Yes, I could watch them for free. As I shared having this gig with a few folks, I was amazed to learn I had more friends than I ever realized. They began reaching out to see if I could let them in at no-cost. I said "yes" to them all. The only real negative aspect to this job was it took me out of the house away from my wife several nights per week and at least part of every weekend. While the extra money was helpful, it could not replace time away from her.

That initial teaching opportunity and movie job experience faded away as my years at Anne Arundel Community College passed. My next notable gig in higher education was at a four-year institution. I was now the number two person in the university relations office at Towson University. As one of Maryland's premiere public institutions of higher learning, I viewed this job as a positive step forward in my career trajectory. More responsibility, higher pay, and a wider array of opportunities to grow professionally. Within a few years of joining the administrative staff at Towson, I began working toward a second master's degree and started teaching part-time within the institution's communication department. I had no idea where any of this would lead. But it felt good. I was busy being challenged and devoting much of my time and energy on worthwhile matters.

The transition from the community college to the four-year university was not a smooth one. Between those two jobs, I took a slight detour to a position outside of higher education. I left the community college to take what was a higher-paying job in the private sector. I was now the public relations director for an international patent searching company operating in Crystal City, Virginia. The whole thing was a mistake. I did not like the work. I did not like the commute. I did not like the feeling of isolation that came with being holed up in an office all day. On top of that, the boss that hired me did not cotton to me all that much. Though the work, mainly producing the company newsletter and trying to expand the company's overall visibility among its current and prospective clients, that I did was adequate, it was clear from the get-go that the boss and I had little positive energy between us. A few months after being hired, I was dismissed. Downsized. It turns out that at the time I was hired the company was going through a rough financial patch. I apparently did not help turn things around enough for it as had been hoped. Several of us were let go. I, being the most recent hire, was first.

On the one hand, I was relieved. But on the other, I was now unemployed. No income other than unemployment checks that only had a limited shelf life. This happened shortly after my wife and I had our first and only child, a girl, Tracy Michele. She was the best part of being unemployed when being unemployed was the last thing I wanted or needed to be. I got to be the "dad" in the best sense of the word with my kid. My wife had her job to go to as well as the extra challenge of pursuing her own college degree. That gave me and my kiddo a great deal of one-on-one time together. Nothing gave me more pleasure. Also, Tracy being Tracy helped me fend off unwanted visits from two old companions: depression and self-doubt. Still, there would be times when Tracy napped that I would sit quietly at the foot of her crib silently crying. My fear of becoming less than successful or respectable in my own eyes and in the eyes of others seemed coming to pass. What the hell was I going to do? The answer, of course was simple yet came with no guarantee of success: search the help wanted sections, send out my resume and letters of application, maintain contact with friends and acquaintances that might know of possible leads or openings. It took me six months to find the job at Towson University.

There have been times when asked about my professional evolution that I did not even mention my brief time at that patent searching company. I figure, what's the point? It did not last long, was not particularly memorable, and did not see me distinguish myself in any way. Final lesson: it was a road I should not have taken. Wrong turn. Much like ordering a different cuisine from the menu only to find it cost too much and did not satisfy a single taste bud. Having said that, miscues can be good, too. Wrong doors can be helpful. This was one of them. It reinforced the idea that for something—anything—to be a positive experience, one must embrace it for the right reasons. For me, I took the job primarily because of the opportunity to earn more money. No small thing, of course, but money, as many have said, is not everything. It did and does not necessarily bring fulfillment. That job was not what I wanted or needed. I did not feel good. The higher education setting was my professional happy place. Campus life. The freedom to not be tied to one's desk. The freedom to connect with a multitude of scholarly men and women involved in stimulating research projects. Then, as part of that, figure out ways to tell the public about the researcher's work that involved working with the press, a profession I continued to respect even though it proved not to be quite as good of a fit for me as I had hoped. Though a small blip on my screen, the job at the patent search company was an important experience. Even though I may not always share it with others, I make a point of using it as a reminder that for all important decisions to have even a chance of succeeding, then the head and heart must be unanimous in their embrace of those decisions or choices.

I spent six years at Towson University. Overall, time well spent. While there, I began feeling a desire to become a supervisor, one responsible for the success of their office as well as the performances of staff members. This is what drove me to begin looking for a new job. Eventually one came along. It was another two-year institution of higher learning—Howard Community College in Columbia, Maryland. While the institution itself was quite solid, the great appeal here was the opportunity serve as director of public relations. My first time as a boss. I felt ready. To a certain extent, even entitled. In retrospect, perhaps I was feeling cockier than I deserved to feel. I had certainly been supervised. Some of the bosses up till then I had I liked better than others. Some were kind and supportive. Some not. This was now an opportunity for me to put some of my dissatisfaction into more positive action by conducting myself toward others in a way I believed to be fair and supportive. Correct whatever perceived wrongs that I had identified. At this new job I had a staff of five. All hard workers. All decent people. All, at times, on overload when it came to the demands being placed upon them to produce promotional material.

I believe I made a positive difference there though, in retrospect, not much of one. The focus of the office as devised by the new boss was oriented toward producing publications. My preference was that we shift things a bit to direct our attention to generating more media coverage. That spoke more to my strengths and interests. Our conflicting visions were a constant topic of conversation between us. A little over a year after stepping into this position I was back to searching for a new job. No hard feelings. Time to seek out something that was a better fit.

Howard County, Maryland, was a good location for me. My parents were close by. My wife, Ida, with whom I had separated and was in the process of divorcing was close, too, thus making it easier for us to share custody with our daughter as well. Plus, the townhouse in which I lived was comfortable and conveniently located to help me meet all shopping needs. These were some of the reasons I had accepted the job in that geographic area. The last thing I wanted was a heavy commute or, for that matter, to relocate.

Time passed. Lots of applications. A few interviews. No offers. Nothing that rang my bell. With each passing week it was becoming harder to brush off feelings of discouragement. Then, one day I noticed an ad from George Mason University, a growing institution in Fairfax, Virginia, that was seeking to fill its position of director of university relations. It sounded good. Yet Fairfax was approximately fifty miles from my home. Would I really want to make that kind of drive primarily on the Washington, D.C. beltway every day? No. But I decided to send in my resume anyway. Maybe I will get lucky and get an interview, I reasoned. More experience at selling myself. That could not hurt. And if nothing came of it, that would be okay, too. Weeks later I received an invitation to come in for an interview. A date was set. This was now the tail-end of 1988. Approaching this, I saw myself as older, more experienced, and hopefully a bit wiser. Better able to give a more positive showing of myself. I met with a committee. It went well. Shortly afterward, I was invited back for a second interview. Down to me and one other candidate. The more I learned of the university, saw of the campus and interacted with its employees, including my prospective boss, the more I liked it. The more I learned of the job itself the more I wanted it. Collectively, it seemed like a place where I could hang my hat for a great many years. Perhaps the remainder of my professional career. Never mind the commute.

I began work at George Mason University in January, 1989. The relationship lasted over thirty years until my retirement. Even beyond my formal retirement. A good run. A respectable run. A relationship with my employer that included its share of ups and downs, times of celebration and disappointment, and significant professional and personal growth. Looking back, I can easily say the "me" that reported to work that first day was definitely not the "me" that left over three decades later.

My first several years of employment there proved to be a mixed bag. Professionally, it was a thumbs-up. Personally, a physical challenge. Given the distance between where I lived and Fairfax, I was traveling nearly one hundred miles every work-day. And that did not include the one night each week I had the communication class at Towson that I was teaching. Yes, the extra money was good. Yes, the added teaching experience was good. But, damn, the wear and tear of all that driving was more taxing than I had imagined. When I was not at work, I was home recuperating from the congestion of traffic. Getting up early. Going to bed early. Trying my best not to fall asleep at the wheel of my car or behind my desk. Giving my daughter the attention she needed and deserved. Singularly, each day was a physical challenge. Taken together, a major burden. So, after all this time, this is when the rat race and I finally came face to face. One aspect of my commute that helped ease my own challenge was my awareness that there were several George Mason employees who traveled back and forth from Richmond to Fairfax—nearly two hundred miles every day, proving the adage that there is always someone who has things worse. Still, I wasn't winning at the rat race.

My roles and responsibilities at George Mason changed over the years depending in large measure on who my boss was and their vision of what I should be doing. Consequently, my roles evolved from being the institution's primary driver of its publicity engine to serving as the President's speech writer to being the university's chief spokesperson to working as a member of the faculty. At times I had people report to me and at times I did not. At times I filled all those roles all at once and other times I had only one primary responsibility. As a culmination, my final years at George Mason I even worked abroad. George Mason had opened a campus in South Korea where I relocated and served, initially, as a member of the faculty, and later was elevated to joint appointments as the campus' chief of staff and dean of university relations.

Thirty years at any one place is a long time. When I arrived at George Mason on my first day, it was not with the notion that this was where I was going to remain until retirement. I figured I would give it a shot and take each month and year as they came. So long as I remained challenged, felt I was making a positive contribution, got on well with others, and was happy there, then I would remain. The prospect of seeking a new job was not necessarily what I wanted, but it was a door that I was not yet ready to close. When I began working at George Mason University, I was nearly halfway through my thirty-ninth year of life. A single parent. Still in search of a job to which I could dedicate myself completely. Not nearly as settled personally as I wanted or longed for. Yes, I had roots in the sense my parents were still alive, and I had a daughter. I had relatives and friends. But even with all that, I was alone. I felt it, too. I wanted roots that ran deeper than merely being grown up and on my own. Yes, I dated. Some of the women I saw multiple times and even with the idea that maybe one of them might be "the one." Bottom line: not one was. Sometimes my fault. Sometimes theirs. Sometimes no one was to blame. As I saw it, given the commute that would come from living in Maryland and working in Virginia, the prospect of finding a person with whom I could build a life were not great. But one thing at a time. When it came to priorities, first, keep trying to be a solid parent, hang onto a fulfilling job, and third, perhaps establish the kind of connection with a woman that dominated so many of my dreams and hopes.

Without question, by the time I walked away as a full-time employee from George Mason in 2019, my bag of memorable experiences was overflowing. The great majority of the folks with whom I worked and interacted were solid and decent and even inspirational. A few were crocodiles. To be expected, for sure, but nonetheless the reality of them did not overshadow what I will label the positive element that largely defined the administration and faculty. The nature of my duties and responsibilities at George Mason—by far, the largest public four-year institution in Virginia—called upon me to connect with literally most everyone who worked there. By then, faculty alone numbered almost 1,400, with many more total employees serving the over 37,000 students. Interacting with these men and women gave me a genuine sense of the university and its multiple parts as well as a deep appreciation of how vital it is for each element to interact with a sense of serving the "greater good" as opposed to serving its own self-interest. Some units and people were better at that than others. Perhaps the main reason I enjoyed serving as the university's chief spokesperson was it gave me a chance to represent and sing the praises of all the professionals I represented and respected. They deserved the goodwill of the media and general public.

In revisiting my time at George Mason, my purpose here is to not simply rehash old times or provide a litany of one highlight after another. I will instead speak to just a few for the purpose of illustrating my experiences and showcase some episodes that greatly influenced my own growth.

The great majority of my years at George Mason revolved around two of the institution's presidents under whom I served: George Johnson and Alan Merten. George Johnson was president at the time I was hired. He was a brilliant, over-powering figure. He was also the person, in my view, who more than any other was responsible for the national reputation that George Mason eventually generated. Many on campus, even highly-respected scholars, found Johnson to be intimidating because of his intellect, the force of his personality, and his temper. I know I did. At the same time, I always appreciated his vision and commitment to helping the university "reach the stars," as he would say. One day he called me into his office and asked me to organize a press conference to announce a new initiative being put forward by the university. After reviewing the main thrust of this initiative and the main points he wanted to communicate, I walked out of his office with a confident assurance that this would not be a problem.

Fast-forward two weeks. President Johnson and I were at the on-campus location of the press conference with several appropriate faculty members. Microphones were in-place. Fact sheets were ready to be distributed to the nearly one dozen reporters who had said they would attend. The appointed time arrived. Nothing. We all waited approximately twenty minutes and concluded that no reporter would be attending our media event. I was devastated and embarrassed. The faculty members we had arranged to participate left, leaving me alone with President Johnson. I had no doubt that he was going to give me a tongue-lashing that probably would take me years of therapy to come to grips with. Instead, as we walked back to the administration building, he put his arm around me and told me not to worry about it. "Sometimes, we can't always control everything," he said. "Thank you for your work on this."

The kindness and grace this man of power showed me at that moment is something I have never forgotten. In the years since, I have found myself to be in positions of authority over others. In trying to be the best leader I could be, I have always kept the memory of this moment close at-hand. Direct others with heart and an open hand. Leadership is about more than simply producing a designated number of widgets. It is also about helping others grow and motivating them to feel positive about who and what they are. The best kind of leaders, President Johnson taught me, are ones who inspire out of love as opposed to fear.

In another instance, I found myself in direct competition with my immediate boss, the professional who had hired me. The man who replaced Johnson was Alan Merten, a dean from Cornell University. He had just settled into the driver's seat of the institution a few weeks earlier. As was customary, the university began making preparations for his inauguration. The new president needed someone to help with his speech for this significant ceremony. It would be his first major address as president. He turned to my boss and me and asked each of us to prepare separate drafts of his inaugural remarks. This, he explained, would help him determine whose style of writing he would be most comfortable with, not just for this upcoming event but for the tenure of his time as president. Neither I nor my boss felt comfortable at all with his directive. We did not appreciate going head-to-head with each other. I did not like being in a position of possibly outshining my boss and she, as a vice president, did not appreciate being in a position of having any part of her access to the president compromised or authority diminished. Both of us knew, without discussing it, this unexpected twist was not going to turn out well for either one of us. We completed our individual drafts. A few days passed when the president made known his decision. With no fanfare, he said he preferred my version. President Merten informed my boss and she passed on his decision to me. Inside, I was pleased. Also, I was concerned about my boss' reaction. I knew she would be upset and understandably so. I was right. Things between us over the ensuing weeks were awkward. But the good news is we were eventually able to get back on track with what had been a positive working relationship. She deserves a great deal of credit for this.

That behind us, it set in motion a most rewarding relationship with President Merten. The two of us began working closely together on his speech. We spent hours in front of my computer fine tuning one draft after another. It put us on path of good will and trust that only strengthened with time. This lasted until President Merten's retirement just a few years before I stepped down. Over the years, members of the press would contact me for comments from George Mason's president on various local and even national issues of the day. At the same time, internally people would ask me to obtain quotes from the President to be used in various promotional pieces. The President trusted me enough to respond to these requests without checking with him first or running by my responses in his name for his approval. The only time I would do that, he said, is if I felt I needed to. To have such a level of trust and confidence from another person made me feel honored and humbled. No other member of his administrative team, to my knowledge, was given such free reign. In the sixteen years we worked together, not once did I ever have to retract any quote attributed to him that I put forward.

So, how did I do it? When people asked me for comments from President Merten, how did I come up with something to say without first asking him? Was I a mind reader? No. But what I focused on with him was being an active listener. I gained a deep sense of his feelings and positions on a number of issues by listening to him at meetings, in conversation with others, and, of course, when the two of us would converse. Also, it was vital that I educate myself as to the issues of the day regarding the university, the Commonwealth of Virginia and higher education in general. Not once did I insert my own views on matters and pretend they were his. As best I could, I put myself inside his head and did my best to communicate as I felt he would. Listening is more than being about the listener. Rather, it revolves around understanding the perspective of others. Perhaps one of the benefits of being an introvert is that it gave and gives one much opportunity to develop sound listening skills. The trick there is to recognize those opportunities and appreciate the value that comes with listening. Sound communication is far more than being able to speak well. The other half of that, which sadly is often overlooked, is being able to listen well—hear and understand.

The one sour aspect of my close relationship with President Merten revolved around the person who succeeded my initial boss after she retired. Being new, she recognized the importance of establishing her own close ties with the President who, within the administrative structure, was her direct superior. As their working relationship evolved, she was never comfortable with the connection I had with him. She saw it as a threat. As a result, she was never sure of my loyalty to her. Her concern was that I might be undermining her authority over me by working at cross-purposes with her vision for me as well as the unit that she directed. Neither was true but this did not ease her concern with me or her uncomfortableness with the relationship I had with her boss. It proved to be an issue between us that never was resolved. Did I contribute to our sour relationship? I tried not to, though I fully recognized the institutional standing I had by being linked to the President. I did not want to lose that. Balancing my link to him and my boss was not easy. The tension, in fact, between my boss and I devolved to a point where hardly a day passed when I did not believe I was going to be fired or dismissed by her. My sense of impending doom only stopped completely when President Merten announced his plans to retire and, several months later, she left the university for a new job.

At the age of sixty-four I began moving forward with my own retirement. President Merten's plans to step down seemed like a good time to assess my own future. It seemed like an appropriate time for me to begin easing my own way out of the door. This thought, initially however, did not begin with me. The credit for that goes to the boss who was not comfortable with my relationship with the President. With his upcoming departure, my interpretation of her suggestion that I retire "now" was that she saw this as an opportunity to rid herself of me, thus removing a key impediment of her having the kind of relationship she wanted to have with whomever might become her new boss. With that, I saw my options as: (1) negotiate with the university to put together the best possible retirement package I could or (2) respectfully decline the opportunity to retire earlier than I had planned and risk having my boss remove me from my job under the justification of reorganizing her department. I opted for option number one.

With the assistance of the office of human resources, my boss and leaders within the university's College of Arts and Sciences—the largest single unit at the institution—it was agreed that I would spend my final year at George Mason teaching full-time in the department of communication. This was an arrangement that was very pleasing to me as it moved me away from what I viewed as intense internal fighting in the wake of the President's departure. I wanted nothing to do with it. Let the sharks fight it out. As a result, generally, the President's retirement had little direct impact on my final months, with one significant exception. I co-produced a large retirement black-tie gala honoring both President Merten and President Johnson and the university's history. It went extremely well. My boss did not attend the gala. That aside, my focus was on crossing my own finish line and beginning the next phase of my life. Interestingly, mid-way through that final year my boss unexpectedly resigned to take a position in the private sector. Apparently, her decision to leave was influenced by issues she was having with several influential academic deans. Her departure did not affect my own trajectory. At this point, my wife, who was already retired, and I were quite looking forward to sharing retirement together.

But a funny thing happened on the way to full retirement. During what I saw as my final months, the university opened a new campus in Songdo, South Korea. With much fanfare, George Mason had become part of what was called a global university that consisted of several institutions of higher learning, including the University of Utah, Ghent University, and the State University of New York. To help make this venture a success, George Mason began recruiting faculty members to relocate there for one, two or even four semesters at a time. While I found this initiative to be interesting, my initial sense was that it was not anything that I would consider. Postpone my retirement—something my wife and I were eagerly anticipating? I think not. Take a giant step outside our comfort zone at this stage in our lives? No way! To that, all I can say is it is funny at times how one day one can be certain of something only to completely reverse themselves a short time later.

The more my wife and I discussed the possibility of relocating to the other side of the planet for five months the more we began warming up to doing something neither of us had ever even considered. The more we talked about it the more we tried to begin identifying reasons not to do it. We got to a point where we could not name one valid reason not to take advantage of this wonderful opportunity and adventure. So, following discussions with the appropriate university officials, including the chair of the communication department, my wife and I found ourselves sitting comfortably in the coach section of our Korean Air flight. Fourteen hours later, we were where General MacArthur was approximately sixty years before: Incheon. I was there to teach classes in public relations and speech. It was to be for one semester only—enough to give us bragging rights with friends and family that we had once lived abroad.

That semester proved to be a wonderful fit for us. The people were kind and patient. The university did a great job of helping make the experience as comfortable as possible. That semester, we were able to squeeze in trips to China and Japan. And my classes were stimulating and fun. At that point, enrollment at the George Mason Korea campus totaled around five hundred students. Not a bad beginning for this international initiative.

Part-way through the semester the chief officer of the Korean campus asked if I would be interested in assuming the position of dean of academic affairs. I was highly flattered and surprised. Me, a dean? It would certainly be a good position to retire on. I said I would be open to it even if it meant extending our initial stay there for at least another two years. Mason Korea's president began talking with key people back at the main campus about a possible appointment. Time passed. The end of the semester approached. Our return home drew near. Finally, word came that while I was worthy of consideration, the top George Mason officials felt that as I had never held an academic position of that rank before, appointing me to such a position would not work for them. Yes, I was disappointed but the prospect of even being considered was most pleasing. Thus, with a great deal of gratitude and sadness, my wife and I returned home. Would we be open to returning there one day? Yes, but the chances of that happening seemed very slim.

We were back home in Fairfax and settling back in when I received a communiqué from George Mason's school of business. Would I be interested in returning to South Korea to teach several business classes? Up till then, the only teaching I had ever done was related to the field of communication: journalism, public relations, and speech.

Business classes on a college level would definitely be a challenge. It would also require a good deal of prep work on my part if I were to come even close to doing a respectable job. Quick conversation with my wife. "Back to South Korea for another one, possibly two, more semesters?" She said, "Yes." I gave the university's school of business a thumbs-up. Quicker than one can say kimchee, we were flying back to a part of the world we had assumed we would never again see.

One big change upon our return was that Mason Korea had a new president: Steven Lee. We had not yet met. That soon changed. The two of us had several conversations about our histories and the overall campus. I found him to be quite engaging. My sense was he had an equally favorable impression of me. Time passed. My business classes seemed to be going well. I was not an expert in this subject by any means, but I managed to keep several steps ahead of the students in terms of sharing and interpreting the information in our textbooks. Plus, my wife and I managed a few more side-trips, including to Vietnam and Hong Kong.

One day I received a request from the President's office for me to meet with him. I had no idea why but was certainly open to it. More chit-chat sounded good to me. The conversation quickly became more than that. President Lee sked if I would be willing to stay on and assume the duties of two new administrative positions he was creating: Chief of Staff and Dean of External Relations. In addition, he said he would be willing to let me continue teaching, but only one class per semester. As part of my responsibilities, I would be second-in-command and would oversee the campus during times he was traveling or absent. I did not see any of this coming. As he shared his vision with me and eagerness for us to work closely together, it was all I could do to keep my head from spinning off my shoulders. I could not wait to share this unexpected turn with my wife. She proved to be as excited as I was. That meant more time away from family and friends back home. At the same time, we thought the opportunity was something not to turn away from.

The next day I informed Dr. Lee that I—and my wife—were on board with his offer. A very happy day. At this point the semester was close to ending. Soon we were back home and began making plans for an extended stay in a land and with a people that we had come to embrace; also, in our minds and hearts, we believed they had come to embrace us. Happy time indeed.

The time in these roles passed quickly and, overall, well. I enjoyed being President Lee's partner. My work ranged from outreach efforts with the community and helping him prepare public presentations to working closely with the staff in a supervisory and, at times, advisory capacity and working closely with faculty as well as my own students. My days were very busy but enjoyable. I found having the kind of responsibility that I had gave me valuable opportunity to try and make a positive difference in the lives of others. For me, at least, it was a comfortable fit. I enjoyed the responsibility, keeping in mind what Robert Ingersoll said of another president—Lincoln—and power. If you want to get a true measure of another, he said, give that person power. What do they do with it? Do they use it to tear others down or build them up? Deceive or instill trust? Fatten their own pockets or create opportunities for others to advance? As best I could, I wanted to use whatever power I had to be that kind of positive force. Such a notion made me realize that all of us, regardless of whatever professional standing we may have, are in positions of power every day. With our spouses. With our children. With neighbors. Our behavior has impact. Our choice, then, is to decide whether we want our impact to be positive or negative. Helpful or hurtful? Loving or hateful?

I do not recall exactly when I began hearing rumblings from faculty members and several contacts back at the main campus in the U.S. about growing concerns with President Lee. His working relationships with folks whom he needed to get on well with apparently were not as positive as they should have been. I approached him about what I was hearing. He confirmed the rumors. "What is going on?" I asked. His explanation was that they were not giving him the freedom he wanted to run the campus as he saw fit. He believed they were crowding him unnecessarily. He felt it best to push back. That made me nervous—for his sake. I asked if there was anything I could do to help. He thanked me but said, "No." He would keep me posted on anything he felt I needed to know. With that, I carried on with my normal duties.

That summer of 2018 President Lee was called by his administrative superiors to travel to the main campus for urgent meetings. Shortly afterward, he left. He never returned. We soon learned that President Lee had been removed from his position effective immediately and that additional personnel changes would soon follow. None of us at the South Korean campus knew what was coming or precisely what had led to his sudden removal. Staff and faculty began bombarding me with questions about what had happened. They turned to me for the inside scoop, only I had nothing to share. Given my close working relationship with President Lee—closer than any other at that campus—I began wondering about my own future there. Would I be removed as well as part of an effort to "clean house and bring in fresh leadership?" The answer turned out to be "yes." I was given the option to remain there, but only in a teaching capacity. My administrative days, it seems, were coming to an end. No explanation was provided other than in lieu of Lee's removal, it was felt that it was best for the campus that I, too, be removed. My official end date in my administrative roles was set for January 2019. I quickly decided to not stay on and teach. Teaching full-time was not anything that was of interest to me at that point. Also, given the abrupt changes, including my being removed without anything close to an adequate explanation other than my ties to President Lee, I felt it best that I remove myself completely from that environment. Let others step in and not have my presence serve in any way as a distraction or be construed as a hinderance to the new leaders. My wife was in complete agreement. So, as I had first arrived at George Mason in January 1989, the symmetry of stepping down completely exactly thirty years later seemed appropriate. With that, my wife and I returned home and began—finally—our new chapter as a fully retired couple.

I confess that leaving under those circumstances left an unpleasant taste in my mouth. I hoped when this day came there would be no regret or clouds with even a hint of darkness over me. The fact I did nothing wrong but was simply caught up in corporate action that has happened plenty of times at plenty of places before in the public and private sectors helped soften whatever hurt I was experiencing. Those feelings soon disappeared as did my anger toward the individuals that set in motion the changes and then ultimately carried them out as they applied to me.

One final note regarding employment at George Mason: my official association with them did not end there and then. In the summer of 2021, I was approached by the Provost's office about the possibility of teaching an online class for them called, "Building Professional Competencies." I agreed and, as of this writing, I am doing that. It is a departure for me as there is no in-person interaction with students. We communicate exclusively online. While I miss the direct connection, I find this—for me—new form of teaching to be satisfying and even fulfilling. I must also note that having the Provost's office reach out to me gives me a small sense of vindication as it was that same office that had ended my administrative duties at Mason Korea two years before. I still consider myself to be retired, but this new gig means I am not quite fully out to pasture yet. I am okay with that.

Through the years, I have left various jobs. Without exception, offers were made to organize farewell celebrations on my behalf. I was always grateful. At the same time, not once did I accept these kind offers. The prospect of such ceremonies brought me back to how I felt—and feel—about being in the spotlight; being the focus of attention. No thanks. In my life I have identified numerous actions that I do not do well. Saying goodbye is one of them. The old song, "Don't Like Good-byes" most definitely applies to me. When my final days arrived, more often than not I simply slipped out the side door and walked away. It is an action that goes back to my childhood. I wish I was better at expressing my feelings at these kinds of emotionally difficult moments. I wish I was a more gracious receiver of kind and heartfelt words and gestures from others. I wish I had felt more worthy of the complimentary expressions of others. I recognize that such behavior on my part possibly smacks of a certain level of selfishness and is unfair to others. I regret that, too. Finally, I recognize that ascribing my behavior in such circumstances as being my nature is not the best defense or explanation. Given the choice between spotlight or exit door, I have chosen the latter. Still, even now, at this point in my life, my inadequate explanation is the best I can do.

In the latter years of my time at George Mason, I began writing books along with a regular blog on communication. Mostly, the books were on some aspect of public relations and/or communication. One was even a compilation of my blog entries. There were also a few workbooks that I co-authored with others. All the books were used for varying lengths of time as textbooks at several colleges and universities in the U.S. One textbook in particular pertained to the function of being an organizational spokesperson or press secretary. At the time I wrote it, no other textbooks on this specific topic existed. My premise was that the most effective press representatives are the ones who are the best listeners. Yes, they should be articulate and honest. But it is vital to their effectiveness that what they say in interviews, speeches, press briefings, etc. relates to the specific questions, concerns, and needs of the intended audience. Without such a connection or purpose being made, the work of a spokesperson will never be as good as it could or should be. Beyond those communication books, I also wrote a children's book and even a humor book. Hardly anyone purchased either one of them. Disappointing, yes, but also not a big surprise. Like my doctorate they were more for me than anyone else. I can say the same for this autobiography. I hope that is of interest to folks beyond me. But if not, then that is all right. I remain grateful for the mountain I had to climb to see it through to completion.

Throughout the years I was fortunate enough to receive a number of honors—some more notable than others. They touched on early efforts in my work as a journalist, my work in public relations, my work as a supervisor, and my performance in the classroom. I was even recognized as alumnus of the year by George Mason's department of communication. Collectively, they all felt and still feel great. They all came in the form of plaques or certificates. Not one, including my academic diplomas, are hanging on any wall in our home. Part of the reason for this is modesty. But mostly it speaks to a deep conviction on my part not to allow myself for even an instant to think any more of myself as a professional—or person—than I deserve; in other words, not allow myself to get a "swelled head." That is a sure-fire road to arrogance—one I have traveled before and one I do my uppermost to avoid. I am a "work-in-progress." Nothing more. As a retiree, I am a retired work-in-progress. Such a self-imposed title may never make it on my wall either, but just the same it is very much branded into my inner core. This keeps me focused on being the best I can be each day rather than resting on whatever laurels or accolades that may have come my way over the years.

Counting my work for the University of Tennessee's student newspaper, my total career in the professional world has lasted slightly over fifty years. By far, the bulk of that time was spent at George Mason University. That place was the venue for my most significant evolution as a worker. It certainly had the most impact on me as a professional as it helped shape my work ethic and gave me greater insight into my own personality, including weaknesses and strengths. Consequently, from it is where I draw so many of life's lessons and much of the criteria from which I judge myself as a functioning adult. Responsible, dependable, occasionally off-track, loyal, generally consistent, collegial. All qualities I may not have mastered but at least strived for with as much effort and even consistency as possible. Primarily at George Mason, upon assessing the way I choose to engage with others, regardless of their rank or level of responsibility, particularly with the passage of time, I can see how I was both my top asset and my worst enemy. The culmination of that dual reality resulted in a university that has not always had a clear idea of what to do with me. When I was active in baseball, I regularly played numerous positions: pitcher, catcher, infielder, outfielder. The very definition of a utility player. Helpful but difficult for others to determine what I was or what precisely to do with me. As the years at George Mason passed, more and more I presented myself in a similar mode. Helpful but difficult for others—particularly those with the power to promote and realign—to assess and place. There was also the matter of my personality as well as my philosophy as it applied to working with and, at times, supervising others.

As an introvert, my inclination is to withdraw, move back to the end of the line when everyone is asked to shift forward. My tendency is to disengage, keep others at bay. Yet I realized that in this professional setting, I could not do that. I had to be actively involved, mingle, initiate relationships. This meant I had to somehow reconcile my personal tendencies/preferences with my professional reality. Was there any way to build and maintain that bridge in a way that I could at least come close to satisfying both of my internal camps? Perhaps. My ultimate solution came down to self-deprecation and humor. That seemed to make the most sense to me. Use those weapons to develop a positive reputation while at the same time keep folks at bay. Make them feel closer to me even if they really were not. If done well, I reasoned, I could navigate my way through each workday unscathed and preventing folks from getting a glimpse of a me that they may not find all that appealing. Light and breezy. I do not defend or make excuses for this game plan or suggest that anyone else should follow it. Generally, it worked for me. But with a price.

One question this raises is: What did I not want people to see? This is a question I raised many times with myself over the years, particularly while on my excursions through my various neighborhoods. What was I trying to protect them from? Me? Themselves? I confess that my response remains imprecise. The quick answer is my "underbelly"—that part of most any living creature's anatomy that represents its area of deep vulnerability. For me, that speaks to my levels of insecurity, feelings of not being good or bright enough. Also, aversion to the inevitable complications that come with possible entanglement and familiarity. Also, to having exposed the contradictions within me that I feared would lead to negative judgement and ultimate rejection. To keep the focus from others diverted, I tried presenting myself on a personal and professional level as an easy-going guy with little or few worries. Such a persona, I figured, would help people see me more favorably than reality dictated. My justification was that people are content with surface relationships. Consequently, by giving them a surface version of me, then I was giving them what they wanted while keeping more than enough of me to myself to give me what I needed. The logic made sense to me. Still does to a certain extent. At the same time, I can see how this persona was not totally honest. I was kidding myself as well as being disingenuous to others.

The surface version of me was jolly, light-hearted. One co-worker even described me once as the "funniest guy on campus"—a descriptive with which I never agreed. Not even close. I purposely kept my conversations light. Sitting in meetings, much of what I would chime in with would be laced with attempted humor, amusing quips. At that moment, people would chuckle or even laugh out loud. It took me years to realize that by doing that on a regular basis I was developing a reputation as a pleasant enough fellow but one that did not always take things as seriously as I should. I learned that in the workplace, people look more to the serious person rather than the quipster. Ironically, I did not see myself as being all that funny or unserious. Still don't. I do see myself as more of a down-to-business person; yet here I was sabotaging myself and not having the insightfulness to recognize it for years and years. In my view, how I was perceived—thanks to me—contributed to my not being considered for various promotions over the years, being invited to participate on various campus projects, or to serve on key committees. The fact I was poor at self-promotion did not help either. At multiple times I would go out of my way to recognize others and purposely playdown my level of involvement in various projects. Yes, sharing credit is a good thing. So, too, is acknowledging the hard work of others. But in an environment where ambition dominates the water, is it wise to come across as non-serious and unambitious? I thought so. I figured the way I acted was the most honorable way to be and the best way to avoid anything close to a spotlight. I believed those higher up the food chain would recognize my strengths and accomplishments despite my outward behavior and attitude. Being amusing, self-deprecating, and talking up others without giving myself equal time may have kept me off the radar screen of the campus community, including the higher-ups, much of the time. Unfortunately, this included times when I applied for promotion. Being overlooked or not afforded the second look that I felt I deserved and had earned left me feeling unappreciated, underestimated, and cynical. On the other hand, from the perspective of others, possibly how I was assessed was fair when applying for high positions, including vice president of university relations—twice. Stepping into that role was my ultimate goal at George Mason. I take full responsibility for not achieving it. After all, I was the one who had adopted the non-ambitious demeanor. I created the menu about me that my organizational superiors drew from when they were called on to determine whether I was worthy of being accepted into their top-tier ranks. It did not happen. It is the one major development in my career in which I feel the least level of satisfaction. But maybe having only one such regret is not bad. Still, in the name of cold fairness, I must acknowledge that there is the distinct possibility that those higher-ups did, in fact, look beyond whatever light-heartedness I put forth, did focus on my professional performance, and still came to the conclusion that I was not best for the promotion I so desired. Such a possibility is not fun to consider but must not be ignored.

Rejection under any circumstance is hard not to take personally—at least on some level. It is easy to accept when the person involved is not liked or respected. But if they are and are still turned away, then that becomes more complex. It cries out for explanation. The rejectors, ideally, should explain themselves. The rejectee should have the opportunity to learn why they were denied, so they can at least have the option of adjusting their behavior, striving to upgrade their resume, or addressing whatever chinks in their armor they may have. Explanation was not provided me, nor did I seek one out. In retrospect I probably should have. But I remember at the time not being up for it. Being told in-person I was not the best candidate for a position seemed like a double-whammy that would not do me any good, I believed. Instead, I carried on and managed to move forward enough to where my wounds were visible only to me.

I fully retired from George Mason exactly thirty years to the month from when I started there (not including the online class I am currently teaching for the university). Nothing like a nice round number as a jumping off point into full retirement. Retirement is a different kind of job. Granted, the pay is not as good, but the hours are so much better. The dress code is far more casual. The fact that the only meetings I have are social is very pleasing, too. And who cares if in the middle of them I drift off to sleep for a few seconds? No one. Finally, so far, I have yet to come across a single person with shark-like ambition in the pool in which I now swim. Let those folks try and feast off others if they dare. My waters are now calm.

Of course, there were also jobs before George Mason. Some I did well at and others just so-so. Sometimes I fantasize about being president of the United States. In the dream I have just a few weeks away from concluding my second term in office. A reporter asks how I would rank my presidency as compared with others who served before me in that position. Even in my own dream my position is always the same: I leave that question to others to decide. The same is true for my many years as a professional. It is not for me to say how well I did or how good I was except that I did my best. In retrospect, no question I could have done better. I do believe I was better at the end than I was at the beginning. My dance at the end was more true and steady than it was at the beginning. I dwelled in the field of communication.

As a professional, was I driven by a need or desire to be at the top of whatever office or organization of which I was part? I hesitate to say "no" because the truth is I did strive for recognition. Realistically, however, the prospect of my literally being president of a campus, top editor of a newspaper or chair of an academic department is not a role that may have been best for me. My comfort-zone resided more in the realm of what I will term "influential foot solider." The person who serves as spotter for those jumping on a trampoline. In the end, perhaps it did not matter if my ambition included being an entity's chief officer. Positive acknowledgement was good enough. Given my feelings about spotlights, an occasional shout-out sufficed. With that, looking back, whatever high level positions I did reach were gravy.

6

Family Matters

I love my family. I love being part of one. I love the potential for security and peace of mind family gives one in life. I even love how we have the ability to incorporate others into our family via such acts as marriage or friendship or adoption as a way of expanding our level of happiness and comfort. Given that, it remains an interesting phenomenon that often the family members we end up being the closest to are the ones we are not closely linked to when we are born. (On the flip side, there are also family members we start out being close to but end up having little, if any, interaction with later in life.) But in terms of expanding one's family unit, mainly I am referring to spouses and children and even grandchildren. I never had any brothers or sisters. When I was born, I entered the world of my parents. Instantly, they were the inner core of my family. Obviously, I had no choice in the matter. Just beyond them were cousins and aunts and uncles and even grandparents. I became an addition to a family unit that was already underway. As is the case in most every family unit, mine grew at times and at times shrank in size. Old members passed on. New ones were embraced and became part of us. Not only by birth but also by choice. The attachment I feel with some of the members is strong. In other cases, not so much. Why? The reason is not necessarily because some are nicer than others. Rather, it revolves around the trajectory or path each member travels. Consequently, we see each other less frequently. They form other attachments. Whatever commonalities we may have shared erode. Yes, we maintain the bond of "family," but the meaning of that becomes looser. Sharing the same family does not guarantee closeness or even compatibility. As is the case in any relationship, that takes work and commitment.

Intellectually, I understand all this to be the case within all families. Emotionally, I wish it were not so. As I grew up, often I fantasized about being close to every one of my family members. It was not until I entered adulthood that I fully realized what a pipe dream that was. Not unlike winning the lottery. There are family members of mine that I go years without seeing or communicating with. We share the same blood line but have little opportunity to pursue other potential commonalities. Others, fortunately, I do connect with more frequently.

I never liked being an only child. I never stopped wishing that I had had a brother or sister with whom I shared a history in a profound way. Even now, I envy those I know who have had that their entire lives. I feel a twinge of pain whenever I hear a fellow adult confess that they are not close to their brother or sister. How sad. A lost opportunity. It is one thing to have cousins with whom I share the same aunt or uncle, but quite another for children—now adults—to have shared the same mother and father—I assume.

Would I have remained close to my brother or sister in evolution from child to adult? Would I maintain regular contact with them these days laughing about our shared memories and helping each other navigate challenges that we each face in our current lives? It is fun to think about. Fun to pretend I would. These days, however, much like an old book, that dream has been largely moved to the back of the shelf. I am in the present when it comes to my family unit as it stands now. I still have the family unit that I was born into as well as the one that I have come to embrace over the years. We all dwell under the same universal tent. How great would it be if one day all of us literally shared a portion of that tent at the same time!

Given my wish for a sibling or two, it is ironic that I had only one child. A daughter. When her mother—Ida—and I married in 1974, we talked about the prospect of having children. We were both young with little money other than our meager salaries and financial assistance primarily from my parents. At first, I declared that I did not want children. My wife said she did. A few years passed and we both changed our minds. I did and she didn't. During those early years she became pregnant. Neither one of us knew it until she miscarried very early in the pregnancy. That day Ida was in a great deal of discomfort. That day we went to the doctor who informed us of what happened. Despite our differences in wanting children, we were both as upset as we were surprised.

Time passed. We were finally in agreement about wanting a child. At this point, I was working at Anne Arundel Community College. Ida became pregnant. The big day came on July 31, 1980. For me, it started out as what would have been a routine day at the office. It definitely did not end up that way. At 5:14 p.m. Tracy Michele entered the world. My parents burst into smiles when I came out of the delivery room to announce we had a girl. Big day indeed. The delivery had gone well and Tracy and her mom were healthy.

When I finally left the hospital that evening to return home, I stopped and bought a box of cigars. Isn't that what new fathers give out when they celebrate the birth of a child? At least that is what I saw done in the movies. Never mind that I had no interest in smoking. Nor did I know anyone who actually smoked a cigar. I ended up throwing the box out at some point. Not the wisest purchase I ever made. Cigars aside, a few days later we brought our daughter home. A new chapter in our lives was now underway.

How does one go about becoming a good parent? Where does one learn how much patience and understanding they will need in their arsenal? Where does one go to acquire a bottomless well of love from which they will draw as they rejoice in every smile made by the child, navigate every sleepless night when that same child cannot seem to stop crying, and endure every moment of worry for their child even when there is nothing to worry about? We were lucky. Our child brought that "bottomless well" with her. Still, at the moment of her delivery, a new weight suddenly appeared on our shoulders that we had never before experienced. It has never gone away. At the same time, this same child introduced a more profound level of joy into our hearts that we had never had before.

To call becoming a parent a game changer feels like a gross understatement. Unfair to the child. Unfair to the reality that this new person carries with them; a hold on you like no one else. Moments before they were a happy expectation. Suddenly, they are a physical presence that is and remains ever-present. All thoughts are directed toward this new person. All actions with them in mind. I found myself never wanting to leave home. Normally on the way home from work, for instance, if we needed something at the grocery store, then it would make perfect sense to make a quick stop so as to not have to go out again later. With Tracy now part of our mix, I would drive straight home and deal with going back out later. Sunday morning, a quick run to the local drug store to pick up the Sunday paper. Now, more often than not, I would take Tracy with me. Also, as she developed her own walking skills, the two of us would take walks together. Quality time indeed.

I have known parents who fall into a pattern of competition in terms of vying for the child's affection. Each tries to outdo the other. I never felt I was competing with Tracy's mom. Nor did I ever feel that I was competing with my father in terms of being a better dad than he was. Rather, I competed with myself. When it came to parenting, I was overwhelmed with feelings of insecurity. Whether it was changing diapers, feeding her, or rocking my daughter to sleep, I never found what I did to be good enough. To my mind, I was not an easy-going parent, particularly in those early days. For me, far too many moments felt like going to bat in the bottom of the ninth with the bases loaded, and our side down by three. So much riding on how well I did. Lots of pressure. My wife, however, seemed more relaxed. She carried an "I got this" aura about her that I both admired and envied. How did she get so comfortable at this parenting-thing? I constantly wondered. Maybe growing up as one of four children helped her deal with the challenges of parenthood with a level of assurance that I lacked.

I remember one day my father and I were on the phone. Ida was not home, so it was just Tracy and me. Dad made a casual comment about me "watching" Tracy. I quickly corrected him by saying, "I am not watching my daughter. I am raising her." I reflect on that exchange now and want to tell myself to "Lighten up, dude." What my father said was just an innocent expression. He meant no harm; nor was he trying to imply anything negative about my parenting skills. Yet there I was. Ready to defend my role and performance. Taking on all comers who might suggest that I was not being an equal partner as a parent.

Like all families, we had our challenges. Tracy was asthmatic in her early years. A few times we had to rush her to the emergency room as she needed assistance in breathing. Fortunately, there were no complications. Also, she eventually grew out of that problem as many children do. Tracy was also a very light sleeper. During her early years she rarely slept through the night. Her mother and I were like zombies. We did the best we could by alternating who would get our daughter each night to hold her, read to her, feed her, change her diaper, or all of the above.

Tracy was still a little girl when her mother and I began having our problems as a couple. Nothing dramatic. Just drifting apart. More and more our social life consisted of her going out with her friends at night and other times me doing the same with mine. Perhaps the fact Ida was nineteen and I was twenty-three when we married contributed to feelings that we had short-changed ourselves when it came to being more social. Still, would waiting till we were older to marry have made a difference in our demise as a couple? Impossible to say but probably not. I remember the day when we sat down with Tracy—now six—and told her that we had decided that we were going to separate. Tracy was stunned. She exploded in tears. My heart broke into a thousand pieces. I have no doubt the same was true for Ida. Seeing our child's world knocked off its axis hurt like hell. So unfair. Not anything she asked for or deserved. Our job was to stay together so our daughter could grow up in a stable environment. But that was not going to happen. We failed us. More importantly, we had failed our daughter. At that moment, I would not have blamed Tracy if she had asked what the return policy was when it came to parents. Of course, there was no such thing. Tracy was stuck with us: a mom and dad who gave her the peace of mind and emotional security that were allowing her to be happy and evolve without negative disruption into the kind of person she was on her way to becoming. But at that moment, we were ripping her security blanket out of her hands.

Fortunately, though we felt we no longer had the desire to maintain a sound marriage, Ida and I were unshakably united when it came to the welfare of our daughter. While we did not want to be married to each other any longer, we were deeply committed to our kid's happiness and overall welfare. That never stopped being our priority as individuals and as a twosome. We decided that Ida would move out but not far away. Once she was re-settled, we would share custody of Tracy and face all the normal challenges that would inevitably come her way, including doctor appointments, sick days from school, meetings with teachers, attending school events, juggling sleep overs, buying clothes, etc. as partners. This meant our maintaining an open line of communication. We were not stepping out of each other's lives. Rather, we simply no longer wished to continue as a married couple. Unlike our vows of marriage, that pledge was never broken. As sad as our break-up was, our commitment to Tracy remains one of the parts of my life that gives me the most pride. I like to think we came together out of love and we ended our marriage the same way. That assessment, however, did not come my way immediately. It followed much contemplation, review, and, yes, walking. Those times when Tracy was with her mother, coming home to an empty house after a walk was not easy. Though I had friends and family, none was able to pull me out of feelings of isolation that, in this case, was not a welcomed fit. My walks took on a double meaning: a chance to reflect—good—but an act that seemed to reinforce my isolation—not good. Still, I realized that what I was experiencing was not unique to me. This chapter in my life would be something I would have to endure or, in my case, walk my way through. And walk I did. Evenings after work. Weekends. I reminded myself that I was an active player in the decision to dissolve my marriage. Being single was the best option. Wasn't it? But much like the dog that actually catches the car, now what? Being single suddenly did not seem so appealing. What now? Those musings arrived shortly after our physical separation.

The day that Ida was going to move out and into her own place was rapidly approaching. How best to do that in a way that would be the least traumatic for our daughter? It would be an upsetting day for us, too, of course. I sat down with Tracy and asked if she would like for her and I to go do something that day so her mother—with the help of friends—could do what needed to be done on her own. Not seeing it happen might be less upsetting. My six-year-old daughter told me, "No," she wanted to be there to help. Instinctively, she knew this was going to be a rough time for her mom and me and wanted to be present to help in any way she could to help ease our pain. At that moment, Tracy revealed to me what a person of courage she was. "We are in this together," was her message. The child was teaching the adults. Her stance inspired me to be part of the transition that day as well. It also reinforced our belief that adults can end their marriage yet remain mutually supportive. Our dynamic as a family was not ending. Rather, it was changing. Tracy's profile in courage was just the first of multiple times she showed the level of inner strength that resonates within her.

Moving day arrived and all of us pitched in to help it go smoothly. Tears were shed. But we survived with an unspoken assurance that regardless of what the future held, the three of us were bonded and that no matter what changes awaited, we were going to be okay. Bottom line: in a strange and unexpected way, it was a good day made possible, for me, in large measure by my daughter.

Without question, I am biased toward my daughter. Her evolution as a person—child to adult—has been amazing to watch. But it has been challenging, too; one that I have struggled with. For starters, our relationship has changed. How we were when Tracy was in elementary school or a teenager or in college is not how we are now. As she has changed, I have needed to adjust how I am with her in order to remain fresh or relevant to her. At times, it has been difficult as a big part of this evolution has been her healthy movement toward becoming her own person and living a life that is independent and removed from mine. That has been a struggle for me, at times. Intellectually, I recognize the importance and innate goodness of her being an independent, free-thinking adult that moves forward toward her own goals and life choices. Emotionally, however, the nostalgia of her being "daddy's little girl" continues to tug at my heart. The core of my inner struggle is to not put that on her. It is my issue, not hers. Tracy is doing what she is supposed to be doing. To that I say, "Great!" Helping support her journey by respecting her independence is not always that easy. I confess that now in my seventies, it becomes even more of a challenge for me. We interact differently now. The frequency with which we connect is also different. We live in different states now. All this, I suppose, is one of the challenges of aging. I, too, have my own life and that is a good thing, too. But as one who is now closer to their own finish line than they are to their starting gate, the reality of my own growing mortality, I find, is placing a greater spotlight on feelings of my vulnerability than I expected. More and more, it is becoming a regular part of my psyche. The good news is, at present, I am handling it. Walks help. Reflection is an aid. But perhaps like a backache or sore tooth, this gnawing awareness of rising vulnerability is a constant presence in my life. It manifests itself in my wanting more frequent interactions with my kid. But as that rubs up against her independent life, that does not happen as often as I would like. I continue to inwardly celebrate the times we do talk and hang-out and do all I can to make them positive experiences for her. And me. More than anyone, as I see it, Tracy represents "proof" that I existed and ensures that my essence will continue after my own eventual passing.

The weeks following my wife's moving day proved to be a time of growth. Within a year, I, too, relocated. This time to a townhouse in Ellicott City, Maryland. Tracy's mother and I now lived approximately a fifteen-minute drive from each other, thus making whatever back and forth was needed with our daughter a bit easier. Ida and I were now officially separated but in little hurry to divorce. As there were no third or fourth parties in our lives, neither one of us felt a need to move ahead right away with dissolving our union or rushed to move forward with formally ending the marriage. That step, we figured, would be taken when the need arose.

It took me months before I plunged back into the dating scene. The ladies I saw were nice enough, but the hard truth is I was a lousy date. Dating is simply something I did not enjoy. I was not particularly imaginative, did not like staying out all that late and much preferred confining myself to my own routine: work, renting movies, running errands, hanging out with my kid. None of those attributes made for a good first impression to women that thought initially I would be worth getting to know. In retrospect, who could blame any of them for not wanting to hang their hats next to mine or even think, "Hey, I'd like to do that again."? Not me.

By now I was working at George Mason University. The heavy-duty commute had forced changes in my world primarily that revolved around Tracy. My parents became more involved in helping her get to school in the morning and making sure she was watched-over after school as well. This was a major blessing as at times the drive home would take literally hours longer than I anticipated. Damn rush hour traffic. My parents, I must say, enjoyed this time with their granddaughter. Tracy proved to be very flexible in terms of adjusting to the new reality that I could not always be counted on to arrive home at a set time despite the fact I tried.

During this time, Tracy began showing impressive signs of independence: preparing a snack for herself after coming home from school, tackling whatever homework she had to do, and developing a supportive attitude toward her mother and I, to cite a few examples. She was still my "little girl," but at the same time was on her way toward becoming her own person: thoughtful, insightful, brave. Rarely was she the kind of child that challenged the authority of her parents or acted-out in ways that could be labeled overly rebellious. Rather, she matured in a quiet way. Determined, too. I found her evolution to be quite awesome. Admirable. She had a nice set of friends but also seemed comfortable with the quiet that comes with solitude. People would ask what she was like. Almost always, I would respond that she was like a younger version of me except she was smarter, funnier, braver, and better looking. People would chuckle at my response not fully appreciating that I could not be more serious. Whatever my positive qualities, in my daughter I saw the making of the kind of person someone like me would aspire to. Times when we disagreed or when Tracy believed I was not being fair, she would speak her mind but do so respectfully and logically. Thankfully, that has not changed. It only made me respect her that much more. That too, has not changed. We took trips together. Enjoyed movies together. Hung out together. She was my anchor as much as I like to think I was hers during the time her mother and I separated. Without realizing it, she helped give me the strength I needed to adjust to life without her mother and even begin searching for a new life partner.

Within the first several years of my time at George Mason, I became involved in a state-wide organization consisting primarily of communication professionals in higher education like myself. At one point, I was even president of the group. Part of the duties that came with this position included organizing and overseeing the group's annual statewide conference. As president, I began reaching out to solicit folks who would be interested in serving on the planning committee for the conference. One call I made was to the head of the public relations office at Northern Virginia Community College. Located in Annandale, Virginia, it was and still is the largest two-year college in Virginia as well as one of the largest in the entire nation. Would he be willing to serve on the committee? He explained he was about to retire, so declined. However, he did suggest I call his publications director—a woman named Jo Medanich—who might be interested. I did and she was. At that time, the planning group was set to meet in Richmond. She and I arranged to ride down there together as we were the only two from the northern part of the state who would be serving on the committee.

Earlier I referenced the moment my parents met. What was it like? What internal bells within each went off letting them know that this new person was significant, perhaps destined to be in their life forever? Whatever it was, those bells made a return appearance within the first half hour or so of our meeting. Our conversation was easy and fun. I found her to be captivating and engaging. The time passed quickly. By the time I dropped Jo off at the end of the day I was smitten. As I drove away after dropping her off, I kept thinking that this is a lady I want to see again. And again. Fortunately, she felt the same way about me.

Driving away from Jo that day, I thought back to months before, after Ida and I had separated, when I was in a short-lived relationship with another woman. She was the very first person I had dated after my wife and I parted. As it had been months since I had seen anyone, I was not sure I would find anyone who might be interested in me. I was delighted. At first, it was bliss as insecurities and fear of being alone seemed to be vanishing. Then, as often happens in budding relationships, things went sour. I was not her "Mister Right" and she let me know it. I returned home feeling devastated. It was not so much because of her rejection, but more that her decision reinforced my own fears about my future and, for that matter, me. Was I doomed to be without a special someone forever? Even introverts need someone to hold hands and cuddle with, yet here I was without anyone and with no prospect that would ever change.

After our break-up, the next morning I had the first panic attack of my life. Tracy was with her mother. I was alone and was suddenly hit with a tidal wave of uncertainty. Fear. Trouble breathing. What the hell was going? Heart attack maybe? Was I about to die right there in my barely-furnished living room? Would "loser" be engraved on my tombstone? I nervously paced around in circles in the living room stopping every few steps to catch my breath. I felt dizzy. Finally, I sat down on the floor. Moments after that I laid down. Still, my breaths were not coming any easier. Was this how I was going to end?

The good news is I did not die. Slowly the feelings of anxiety subsided. I took an endless series of deep breaths and finally began regaining my equilibrium. I do not recall how long the whole episode lasted. While I was not sure what had happened, at least whatever it was seemed to be over. I slowly rose to my feet and took a seat on the sofa. Should I call anyone? Who? What would I say? I just got dumped by someone and am upset? No thanks to that. I remember reflecting on that internal dialog and chuckling. The fact I was still caring about what others thought of me had to be a sign I was okay, or at least on my way to getting back to normal.

Months and multiple dates later I met Jo. Still alone but no more panic attacks. I had either not found anyone to date more than once or anyone who wanted to date me more than once. Welcome to the dating scene. Who needed it besides me? Who did not want it besides me? I was friendly enough with women. Generally, we got on well. But what I learned about me during this time is that I entered the dating scene with the greatest of reluctance. In fact, it was more out of a practical necessity than any kind of primal hunger. At the end of most days and work weeks, I found myself just as content—if not relieved—to watch a rented movie at night and then call it a day with an enjoyable book than get dressed up and adapt a persona that was more forced than not. Such a struggle was far more about me and had nothing to do with any of the ladies that I socialized with. The ladies I did date were nice. But the hard truth was, now, in my early forties, I was still that kid who sneaked out of his cousin's party rather than stay and mingle. I was still that kid who so often opted to stay in on Saturday night rather than go out carousing with my high school buddies. When it came to dating, in many ways I was that kid who went for long walks on summer days to my favorite drug stores to look at magazines rather than seek out the company of friends. Yes, at times I was lonely and sad about my circumstance. But, generally, not enough to do much about it. I was a homebody who longed for another body to share a home with. But making the effort to woo and win over another body was difficult for me. Sure, I wanted someone wonderful, but who out there would be willing to snuggle up to someone who, in my view, registered on the low end of the fun-scale?

This leads me to Jo and that day we met to share a ride to Richmond. What was the big deal about this native of Texas anyway? Like me, she was a divorcee; parent of one daughter; an only child; getting over a serious relationship; worked in higher education; shy but engaging; cautious when it came to others; at times, not as self-confident as she would have preferred; vulnerable; hoping to connect with a special someone with whom she could spend quiet nights. Also, she enjoyed going to the movies, was open to travel, protective of family and friends—more traits that I shared. The drive down and back went quickly and well. Conversation was easy. Nothing seemed forced. Her smile was magical. Her manner that day was cool and, yet warm. While at the meeting we attended there in Richmond, I found myself stealing glances at her non-stop. I could not but wonder if this is how it was like when my parents met at that party many years before. I confess that the thought of wondering if we might end up like my parents—married—made a quick cameo in my head. I quickly dismissed it yet could not deny its unexpected appearance.

Jo and I talked on the phone. We met for lunch. We began dating. But it was not easy. She lived in Fairfax, Virginia, very near where she and I worked. I lived in Ellicott City, Maryland. I had a child not quite a teenager. Jo, too, had a daughter but one that was in her early twenties, in college, and much less dependent. We lived over fifty miles away from each other—a drive that I made every week day for work and I did not cotton to the notion of increasing the number of commutes each week. Did I mention that moving forward in a relationship was not going to be easy? But move forward we did just the same, knowing full well that overcoming the logistics of establishing a successful relationship would be a formidable undertaking. Even with that, neither one of us fully appreciated the physical and emotional depth of the challenges that were on the horizon. Looking back, all the signs were there that the odds were very much against us. Choosing to remain friends or even colleagues rather than become a romantic twosome would have made a great deal more sense. But as the song says, "fools rush in where angels fear to tread." We moved forward.

We took turns staying at each other's houses. It was a nice enough arrangement but after a while did not seem enough. From time to time we would express our frustration at not being able to spend more time together, but the conversation did not go beyond that. Every so often we also took out our mutual frustration on each other. That was never fun but fortunately those moments did not last long. I liked where I was living even though the commute remained far less than ideal. Being in Ellicott City, however, meant being close to my parents who were both beginning to show signs of being less independent. Being in Ellicott City meant having regular interaction with my daughter. I did not want to give that up, nor did I want to jeopardize her regular contact with her mother. Jo preferred Fairfax. I was very sympathetic to that to the point of seeing how my moving there would be a benefit to my life in several key ways.

One Saturday evening we were watching television at my place. Lost in the show, not saying all that much. The show ended. Silence. I looked over at Jo and asked her to marry me. It is not anything I had planned. I did not wake that morning thinking, "Okay. Today's the day!" I had not given any thought to some grand romantic gesture such as a fancy meal at a fancy restaurant or being at a ball game and having my proposal flashed across the score board in front of thousands of cheering fans. Rather, I was there with this woman I had come to love spending a weekend evening in a way that we both preferred. It felt good. It felt ideal. It felt like something I wanted to make last forever. It was as if my inner self could see what was happening and thought, "Well, if you are not going to say anything, then I will." It stepped forward and asked for this other person's hand in marriage. Simple. Direct. Jo looked at me and said, "Yes." Her response was as simple and direct as my question. At the same time, very much like my question, her answer was profound. In an instant, our lives had changed forever. Our smiles turned into laughter. The laughter into hugs and kisses. There is no better feeling than the feeling that comes with taking action that feels right because it is right. That moment belonged to us. Nobody else. We did not immediately start calling family or friends. We did not climb onto any roof top to shout our pledge to the world either. Rather, we embraced the moment as we did each other. This moment in our lives was for us. We would share it with others later.

The time between that evening and the day we wed contained a number of twists and turns for both of us. Yes, we were on the same page about wanting to share our future. Our challenge revolved primarily around timing and logistics. In terms of timing, her acceptance of my proposal was to be wed in summer, 1993. Then there was the matter of housing. Where would we live? I owned a townhouse in Maryland. Jo had her single home in Virginia. Her home was very close to where she worked and, for that matter, to where I worked, too. Plus, Jo made clear that she did not want to have to deal with driving on the capital beltway every day as I had been doing. Who could blame her? So, the question of where we would live—at least initially—was clear. Her place. In my head, that made perfect sense. I could put my townhouse on the market and hopefully within the coming months it would sell. That was the head-part of my thinking. But the heart-part had a difficult time giving it a similar thumbs-up.

For one thing, there was the matter of Tracy. Her mom and I were doing well in terms of sharing our daughter and co-parenting. Tracy was happy and seemed to be comfortable with the situation of her parents. She knew we were actively involved in her life. Also, she was still a few years away from high school but was making a good number of friends at school. We did not want to disrupt that if it was at all possible. Moving her to Fairfax would mean just that. Either Tracy would have to live with me or with her mother. Ida would be quite upset if she was not able to see Tracy as often as she had been doing. I would be, too. This was a festering issue that tugged at my heart. At this early point, I could see the real possibility that I would be having to make a big adjustment.

And then there was the matter of my mother. At this point, dad was dealing with his cancer. He was not doing well. Without saying it out loud, we knew how things with him were going to go. Mom was happy for me and my plans with Jo. She told me that she felt Jo was a good "catch." In the same conversation, however, she also told me that she did not want me moving to Virginia. Shortly after that, Tracy's mom said the same thing. Yes, Ida was happy for me. But her main concerns revolved around Tracy. Tracy, she reasoned, was happy and doing well. My relocating to Northern Virginia might jeopardize that. That was the last thing I wanted as well. I broached the topic with Tracy. She was happy with our current arrangement. "Why can't we keep things as they are?" she asked. Then there was Jo. We continued alternating going back and forth between our homes. We were enjoying it less and less. Our stress levels were on the rise. Also, was it my imagination or was rush hour traffic congestion on the capital beltway getting worse? My head was insisting more and more that I officially move to Northern Virginia. Yet my heart was feeling tugged at like never before to remain in Maryland for the sake of my mother and daughter. What made this whole situation particularly sensitive is that, as I saw it, all the players on the field were "good guys:" my soon-to-be-new-wife, my daughter, my mother, and the mother of my child. All were folks that I wanted to please especially since they all had perspectives that made sense to me. I was in the middle. More accurately, I had placed myself in the middle. The result was a great deal of anxiety on my part. A big part of my nature revolves around pleasing others. Yet here I was, feeling like I was not pleasing anyone, including me. Surrounded by these vital people yet feeling very much alone. Just because it was a position that I had put myself in did not make it any less stressful.

Did I share my feelings with anyone? Did I let any one of these people, particularly my wife-to-be, know that inside I was feeling tied up in knots? Not me. I did not want anyone to worry. I did not want to disappoint anyone. I did not want anyone thinking I was not sympathetic to their perspective. Even more to the point, I did not want to make anyone angry with me. I believed they were all looking at me for assurance, to ease their concerns that I was not going to do what they did not want. The fact is I did want to please them all. Walks I took during this time were dominated by trying to come to grips with the conflicting challenge of wanting to slide into a happy and comfortable new marriage versus going against those closest to me.

Time passed. No resolution. My father's condition worsened. My mother's feelings of vulnerability grew. Tracy and my ex-wife kept looking to me for reassurance that all would remain the same: my continuing to live in Maryland. Jo believed the matter had been settled and that I was committed to relocating to Northern Virginia. As all this progressed, my birthday was rapidly approaching. Jo hinted that she had big plans to celebrate but it was all going to be a surprise. The reality of organizing whatever it was going to be gave me much-needed reasons to smile at something—at least inside. I had not been doing much of that lately. The day before my birthday Jo and I boarded a train to New York City where Jo treated me to several nights at a ritzy hotel in an equally ritzy suite, a Broadway show, and a New York Yankees-Baltimore Orioles baseball game. Plus, being in New York City, there was lots of sight-seeing. It was fabulous. Except for the arguing. That revolved around the subject of our future. I tried sharing my concerns about moving to Virginia. This was a surprise to Jo who, thanks to me, had been led to believe by word and deed that I was totally on-board with it. I felt I was but at the same time I did have misgivings. I do not remember our exact words but I am sure she became quite upset. My reaction was less than adequate. I did not explain myself nearly as well as I should have or needed to. I was now in the doghouse big time and the fate of our relationship seemed in-question when just days before it was rock-solid.

Arguments or misunderstandings are never fun. I have spent so much of my life trying to avoid them. Skirt around potentially thorny issues. Talk about anything but what needs to be talked about. My experience is that never works. One would think I would have eventually learned the truism that ignoring tough issues only makes matters worse. Say what needs to be said, but do so with respect, honesty, and sensitivity. Do not hold back and trust in the innate goodness of both parties that they will eventually seek ways to agree or at least reach common ground. I fancied myself a decent communicator yet not facing awkward or difficult topics when needed was not an example of effective communicating. In those instances, I fell short more often than I care to admit. My walks at this point turned more into moving pep talks. I could do this, I told myself. More to the point, I had to.

Thankfully, cooler heads often have a way of prevailing in times of stress. Such was the case with us. By the time Jo and I returned home we were no longer bumping heads. At the same time, I still had my issues with the other "ladies" in my life: daughter, mother, ex-wife. They still had their expectations of me. I needed to have the kind of conversation with each that, by nature, I usually did my best to avoid. My marrying Jo was not a problem. But what each preferred is that I do so and remain in Maryland. If I was going to keep Jo in my life, then I needed to be upfront with those three about what I was going to do to make sure I did not lose her.

    I began with Tracy. She was in middle school with high school now just around the corner. Doing well. Enjoying her friends. Active in various school activities. Impressive grades. Comfortable with the sharing arrangement that her mother and I had settled into. I shared with Tracy my feelings about Jo and desire to be with her. At the same time, I shared my concerns of not wanting to do anything to disrupt her happiness or do anything to make her doubt my commitment to her. Tracy told me that she loved me and knew I loved her. She wanted me to be happy. If I needed to relocate to Northern Virginia, then that would be all right. She knew the two of us—daughter and dad—would always be okay. With that, so many of my misgivings began to disappear. So much of the guilt I was feeling began to proceed to the nearest exit. Still, this had to be a tough conversation for Tracy. Like me, she appreciates routine. A large part of her—as is the case with me—is change-averse. My marrying Jo would disrupt her current status quo. For us to establish a new routine that may not be as comfortable or good as the one we were currently in—at least not at first—would require adjustment. There was still the reality of us: father and daughter. At the same time, that reality was about to be placed in a new circumstance. Tracy would remain a resident of Maryland and become a visitor to Virginia in her times with me. Life, as has been said so often by others, is a series of changes. Our conversation was about that change—a new chapter in my life to which Tracy had to adjust. Only a few short years before, her mother and I had introduced Tracy to a life-altering change. Though not quite as traumatic, this was a new one. Still with impact. But now it was me who was the author. Another moment of courage from my daughter. Tears were shed. But heartfelt hugs, too.

    There is no one who has been a greater source of pride for me than my daughter. As it is in many close relationships, Tracy and I have had our ups and downs over the years. Stretches of time when communication between us was scarce. Bolts of anger shooting back and forth between us. Times when I have infringed on her space. Times when I have over-hovered. It has taken me years to get a better handle on that, particularly since it remains my desire to connect with her every day. Tracy is a fiercely independent person. Only in recent times have I learned to embrace this key aspect of her. Tracy remains committed to growth and personal and professional advancement.

Yes, her well-being and happiness are paramount to me. Also, I confess, her approval. Am I a good dad? Have I done right by her? In my mind, I am never totally sure. Several years ago, the two of us had a conversation that helped ease my insecurities. Tracy told me that she has come to recognize that there was never a time in our relationship when I did not give her my best. I may not have always given her what she needed at specific times or been perfect, she said, but there was never a moment when I was not giving her all that I had and have to offer. Not a day passes when those words of hers do not resonate within me. It helps keep my insecurities as they relate to fatherhood at bay.

At the time I was struggling with the prospect of moving to Virginia and letting Tracy live full-time in Maryland with her mom, I was reminded that Tracy was going to leave me eventually no matter what I did. From that time, in five or six years she was going to go away to college to begin living her life without my daily presence anyway. Consequently, I should keep doing what I need to do to remain close to her, but at the same time live my life. She is going to be living hers. She and I would be okay. Such a reality-check helped me enormously.

I then sat down with Ida. I have always found her to be pragmatic and wise in a cool way. Not one to lose her head. Yes, she has her share of insecurities, but none that seemed over the top or worse than anyone else's. She was also highly protective of her daughter. That gave comfort because her daughter was mine as well. I trusted her. I shared with Ida the highlights of my talk with Tracy. We agreed that it would be best that Tracy's primary living address would be with her in Maryland so as not to disrupt her schooling and social life there. For both of us, Tracy's happiness and sense of security were our top concerns. In terms of my seeing Tracy, I was welcome to visit her as often as was practical during the week and have her stay with Jo and me in Virginia at least every other weekend. Despite our separation and divorce, I have always considered it important to maintain a bond with Ida.

My mother was next. At this point, she was a widow. But she was still independent. She could still drive well enough to run to the grocery store, visit her sisters, and even go to the local bingo hall on Saturday nights. After dad's death, having me close by gave her peace of mind. I told her of my plans to relocate. She understood. Still, she did not want me to move. We agreed to agree to disagree. The fact I promised that I would see her at least once every week helped.

I kept Jo abreast of each of these conversations. Her blessing was paramount. Essential. With my talk with my mother over, Jo and I sat down to assess the entire situation and determine what this meant for our immediate future. The fact those steps had been taken and went as well as they did was a big step forward. At the same time, Jo and I knew the two of us still had miles to go before we could think of resting. One issue that remained was my townhouse. It was still on the market. I felt I couldn't totally move to Virginia until it was sold. Plus, Jo and I had agreed initially to marry in the coming summer. I believed I needed to maintain at least a semi-regular presence there to ensure the remainder of Tracy's school year proceeded with little disruption. Jo said she would travel with me to and from Maryland as much as she could. Finally, there was also the matter of our initial agreement that we would wed in the coming summer. Jo now wanted to move that up to the fall. At this point, fall was already underway. If we did that, it left us with very little time to plan any kind of special ceremony.

For the first time in my life I used in a serious way the word "elope" in a sentence that applied to me. Jo and I even began talking about reaching out to a local justice of the peace. Why the sudden urgency? I was not totally sure then. Now, looking back, I suspect for Jo, it came as a way of removing any doubt as to our mutual commitment. Overtures were made to folks with the authority to marry couples. A date was selected. November 3. A weekday. Then, a week or so before our big day Jo said she wanted to be married in our local church that we occasionally attended. Fortunately, the minister, a friend of ours, said he was free to "do the honors." The wedding party consisted of our daughters. (One of my cousins had been nice enough to drive Tracy down to serve as my best person.) One would be hard-pressed to name a wedding ceremony more low-key than ours. Nevertheless, Jo and I emerged as husband and wife for the second and, we hoped, our last time. Afterward, we went out to dinner at a local restaurant and then spent our wedding night at one of the nicer hotels in our area. The next day it was back to work for the both of us. It was then we shared our big news with our colleagues and office friends. Naturally, everyone was surprised. Even though both Jo and I would rather have avoided the hoopla, we appreciated the good wishes. We were happy, too, but only in what I will describe in an off-kilter way. Being Mr. and Mrs. Daniel Walsch was great. But then there was the reality of my still needing to travel back and forth from Virginia to Maryland several times per week. Jo and I were married but not settled. Not nailed down. Thus, our beginning was not smooth. It felt odd to travel to Maryland and spend a night or two alone in my townhouse. It felt odd leaving the office and driving directly to Maryland to see Tracy and/or my mother and then not return to Virginia until three or four hours later. This was not how newly-weds should be living. It was not how I, as one of those newly-weds, wanted things to be. Jo felt the same. Being married was supposed to make things different. Only, for us, it didn't. At least not in a positive way. Before November 3, we talked of how our lives would be different once we were married. Now we were married and our schedules were largely the same. Juggling two homes in different states. My being on the road far too much. More like two individuals rather than a couple. We were happy to be wed but not happy with our marital situation. Yes, I was married but I did not feel as married as I wanted.

That first year of ours was rocky. At best, we found our rhythm only in spurts. Newly-weds, regardless of their age, need time to adjust. Get used to each other. Get comfortable sharing a refrigerator, washer-dryer, bathroom sink, and, yes, a bed with each other on a full-time basis. Embrace running for each other. Running errands with each other. Getting dressed and undressed in front of the other. Above all, giving total acceptance to each other and establishing mutual trust that will last a lifetime and beyond. In our first year there was hardly any of that. For us, that first year was nearly a non-starter. Tension. Little time for relaxation. Misunderstandings. Big mistakes. Errors in judgement. Collectively, enough to make each of us wonder if we had made a serious mistake. As much as we believed the other was wonderful, we both doubted whether our marriage should have happened at all. At times I felt the pull of living in Maryland was too strong. Thus, given the demands that we faced we mused that maybe marriage had not been the best course of action. The doubts—just a few months in the making—grew to where each of us shared them with others. Some of those "others" even advised that we dissolve the union and move on. But we didn't.

Why not? Why didn't we call it off? Life is too short to spend so much time feeling tense and unappreciated and misunderstood and wary. But it is also too short to live life not feeling emotionally safe and appreciated and embraced and happy. For us, the answer was found in ourselves and in each other. Even in the worst of our early times, we both sensed that. The problem was we had only experienced it in snippets. But those snippets were good enough to give us the strength to hang in there with each other. Neither Jo nor I wanted to be divorced a second time. Through marriage counseling, couples therapy and even our own soul searching, we realized that there was a reason we married in the first place. That reason—love—was worth fighting for and building on even if it meant, at times, we were each other's opponent. Jo is a passionate person. Fiercely loyal. Singular in thought when it comes to knowing what she wants. Willing to stand her ground when others are ready to walk away. Surprisingly strong and determined. At the same time, within her is a well of doubt and even insecurity that resides only just beneath her surface. A fear of being hurt. I have come to learn that does not make her weak or anything resembling a pushover. Rather, it illustrates the inner core of her strength as she is unafraid to show her emotional underbelly. Every day she shows all sides of herself because being honest in such an uncompromising, unrelenting way is the only way she knows how to be. Take it or leave it, she communicates. Every day I choose her. Doing so is a constant reminder to myself that my judgement to reinforce my commitment to her—even if I do it imperfectly at times—remains intact.

Jo and I took a deep breath and slowly began moving forward. Yes, there were still bumps. Rough patches. Moments when we both overflowed with exasperation. Times when we wondered if the grass really was greener somewhere else. But those times slowly but steadily grew further and further apart. Feelings of unconstrained contentment began becoming the norm because each day we took time to remind each other of our feelings for one another. Now, over thirty years later and still counting we have gotten damn good at it. Does that mean we never argue or hurt each other's feelings? Hell no. No doubt that will never change. Stumbles will always happen. But so, too, will our reaffirmations and day-in and day-out intermingling. I recognize, to some, this all may sound mushy. Maybe it is. At the same time, it also is our reality. It is the glue that keeps us unified. We are at peace with our need for each other. As for myself, I have finally recognized Jo for what she is: the great love of my life. In coming to that conclusion, I have finally embraced the notion that because of that truism, I devote each day to treating her accordingly and behaving in a way that reinforces that.

Counting both marriages, I have been married nearly fifty years of my life. If asked, one significant piece of advice I would give to anyone contemplating marriage or currently married is to not allow themselves to get hung up on being "right." In my first marriage and in the early years of my second, whenever my spouse and I argued, my primary objective devolved into wanting to win; best my wife. My goal was not just to gain recognition as the winner of our head-butting. It was to be acknowledged as being "right" in whatever position I was taking. At some point, I came to the realization that such a designation not only got me nothing, more importantly it did nothing for my spouse or us as a couple. Being "right" or one-upping one's spouse is not the point of interactions between a couple. The point is to get along; continuing to do what is necessary to further strengthen the union; working for the greater good. This means making your priority "us" rather than "me." This means interacting in a manner that does not lesson your partner or make them feel less than they are. This means not trying to best them in an argument but instead communicating with them in a way that focuses on mutual understanding and respect. Doing what you can to ensure they feel positive about themselves and the two of you. Serving the concept of "couple" and not striving to feed one's own ego. Granted, this is not always easy to do, especially when emotions are running high and one's feelings have been hurt. I do not do it well all the time, but with age I have come to appreciate the thought of Socrates, who came to the conclusion late in his life that, of the two, it is better to suffer injustice (or pain) than to inflict it. I do not wish to hurt—physically or emotionally—my wife. What I do want is to elevate her. One important way I do that is not trying to be "right" when we argue but point my efforts toward making sure we do not allow ourselves to get knocked off-track from the destiny that we pledged to share on the day we married. Such thinking, I have also found, applies with any disagreements one has with those to whom they are close. I understand not everyone either agrees with this line of thinking, recognizes it, even sees it as a way of contending with conflict with a loved one, or is able to put it into practice every time they are caught up in the "heat of the moment." I get it. Purposely making oneself vulnerable is not fun or easy. For me, however, I have found that even if I am the only one following such a strategy, in the case of Jo and me, those times when we do have heated disagreements, the two of us emerge from the experience still on the same path and often more committed than ever to remain that way.

As Jo and I slowly began reversing our trend of taking one step forward and three steps back, our roles as children of aging parents began demanding more of our attention. From Texas, Jo's parents lived in Amarillo. In my case, my father had passed one year before our wedding and my mother continued making a go of it in Ellicott City. Jo's father took ill. With his slide her mother became more dependent, less certain of her ability to continue being the kind of independent person she had been her entire life. The slippery slope they were on led Jo to step down from her job and employment all together and to move back to Texas to be the primary caretaker of her father and, to a lesser extent, mother. In the meantime, I remained in Virginia, carried on with my job and continued being an active presence in the lives of my daughter and mother. As only children, Jo and I were doing what we did out of duty. Our parents had taken care of us. It was our turn to look after them. Sadly, Jo's father eventually died leaving her mother alone and without the security of having the life partner on whom she had counted for decades. The decision was made to relocate her to a senior living facility where she could still have a level of independence while being surrounded by staff and other residents so as to not feel isolated or not cared for. Jo remained in Texas to oversee this transition.

As for me, I increased my travels to and from Maryland. Tracy was active in an array of school plays. Mom required an ever-increasing amount of attention. This was made quite clear when one day while backing her car out of her driveway she backed into the one tree that was situated in the front yard of her house. No more driving. This meant arrangements had to be made to ensure her needs continued to be met. This called for more visits from me. Getting groceries, taking her to the doctor, taking her shopping, and even taking her to Saturday night bingo when friends were not able to do so. Happy to do it though I found it all to be emotionally and physically draining. The tranquility of staying at home grew more appealing by the day. Also, when possible, I squeezed in walks around the neighborhood. I needed them still.

Jo returned from Texas. Did we pick up where we had left off? Our evolution as a married twosome, generally, continued along a positive track. At the same time, my trips to Maryland escalated. With each visit I could see my mother was becoming less sure of herself. More tentative in how she carried herself. This included her ability to communicate, tend to her own needs such as preparing meals for herself, doing laundry, and taking care of her finances. Once an extremely proactive, efficient person, she was now becoming more lethargic and even passive when it came to her life. I started looking at senior homes where she could relocate. I found none to be acceptable. None were good enough for her. Far too many struck me as places where old people went to die under the guise of being well taken care of. The prospect of leaving her in any of those facilities was heart breaking. Yes, they all had a community center or community room of some sort. From what I saw, however, most of the residents were holed up in their rooms either staring blankly at their tv sets or napping. None of the places were like Club Med despite what was portrayed in any of the brochures.

Jo and I put our heads together. It did not take us long to identify a solution: have her move in with us. The idea seemed so simple. Straightforward. Logical. Yet a very big deal. Adding a third person into our eco-system would change our rhythm. At the same time, we believed, it would make things better. I would have more peace of mind. My mother would, too. There would be less driving to and from Maryland. With Tracy now away at college in New York City, Jo and I could devote much more of our time and energy to becoming the kind of couple we wanted to be. Mom needed no convincing. The logistics of making it happen went quickly. My mother was now living with us.

The first months and even year or two of this new arrangement were easy enough. But then my mother's mental capacity began to deteriorate. Alzheimer's. No turning back from that. At first, her mental decline was slow. Yes, she was forgetful, but only slightly. Mom had the ability to smile when smiled at, nod when spoken to and laugh when folks around her laughed. All seemed normal. On the surface, she seemed normal. It was her way of disguising her ever-increasing fogginess. But then her decline quickened its pace. No longer being what she used to be became far more obvious. She needed more help with her food. Eating. More help with her physical hygiene. More help with her walking. Getting dressed. More watching over in-general. As her end approached there were no complaints from her. No outward drama. Mom was pleasant as she drifted away from her world. At times, she was not even sure who I was. The first time she talked with me as if I were someone other than her son was jarring. But I knew this about her. Wherever she was in her head, that is where I was, too. Jo embraced that strategy, too. Our challenge was to give mom love and acceptance. No anger. No feelings of guilt. We looked at her and recognized that might be us sometime in the future. As a result, we did our best to treat her as she would want to be treated. And as she deserved.

Mom's death was quiet. At the end she was in the hospital on a life support machine. The doctors assured me there was not any chance of her regaining anything close to the state of mind she used to have. In fact, there was no chance of her even regaining consciousness. I gave them permission to unhook her from the machine. Within minutes she died. Quiet. No pain. Gone. Dignity intact.

She had lived with Jo and I for five years. To this day I give thanks for that time. I also remain grateful to Jo for being so open to taking-in mom. Our experience with my mother was a powerful bonding time for us. Inadvertently, it proved to be a lasting gift from mom to us. Within months of my mother's passing, an encore experience began to appear on the horizon regarding Jo's mother. Yes, she had a very nice set up in Amarillo. But the fact is she was lonely and did not have nearly as many visitors or social opportunities as she or we had anticipated when she first moved into her living facility for seniors. Given that, the prospect of having her move in with us was practically a foregone conclusion. Of course, we would take her in. Jo and I joked about being in "The Mom Business." But we were very serious. Approximately one year after my mother died, Jo's mother moved in with us. She would remain in our care for slightly over six years. She, too, became a victim of Alzheimer's. The circumstances of her passing were a bit different than that of my mother. She died in our home. It was evening. Jo and I could tell that her end was near. Jo asked me to go to bed as she wanted to be alone with her mom during the final hours. I honored her request. A few hours later, Jo woke me with the news that her mother was gone.

With the passing of Jo's mother, we experienced our own version of the empty nest syndrome. Suddenly the house was totally ours. We were free to come and go as much as we wanted. A nice feeling but at the same time a tad unsettling, too. This so-called freedom was the result of something neither one of us wanted. Now Jo and I had one more thing in common: we were both without parents. Such a reality did not necessarily change how we viewed life in any kind of dramatic way. Rather, it reinforced our belief that with the passing of our parents, we moved that much closer to our own finish lines. A sobering thought, for sure, but at least for me, one that did cause me to try and wake each morning like Ebenezer Scrooge after being visited by the ghosts of Christmas past, present and future and become "as good a friend, as good a master, and as good a man as the good old city knew." This remains my constant goal. Each day, it is first on my personal "to-do" list. I will leave it to others to judge how close I have come to achieving that end.

In addition to family monikers as "son," "cousin," "grandson," "nephew," "husband," and "father," I have added "father-in-law," "step-father" and "grandfather" to this list. Each serves as a great source of pride—not because of the titles themselves but rather the people themselves who made them possible. Each is solid when it comes to their commitment to decency. My primary complaint with them all is none of them live all that close by. We are in Virginia and their home addresses range from Texas to New York. It makes in-person connections all the more challenging. This makes me grateful for "Zoom" and "FaceTime" on our iPhones and computers. This is especially true as it applies to our granddaughter, Madison. "Pure joy" is the best way I can describe her. As much as anyone in my life, when we are together—even after an extended time has passed since our last time together—it is as if we were never apart. How great is that? How lucky am I? Soon young Maddie will be a teenager. I cannot wait to watch her intellectual and emotional growth in the coming years. I will keep doing my best to be part of it.

Age does not release one from day-to-day responsibilities such as paying bills, putting food on the table, being a decent parent if blessed with children regardless of their age, being an honorable friend, being a loving life partner to another, being a responsible citizen, etc. If anything, it highlights the duty of striving to achieve these objectives as consistently as possible. If anything, it clarifies one's path as a person. None of this, of course, eases the challenge of meeting life's future turns and twists and hurdles. I do not necessarily like raking leaves now any more than I did before. But when doing it, even with reluctance, I try viewing it as a small way of helping others and adding to the greater good of our world. The same, in a far more pronounced way, holds true when it comes to reaching out to others. Checking in with family members and friends is an act I find myself doing more than ever before. My introversion remains very much part of who I am. But staying connected with those who have come to comprise and even define my life makes me feel better and, hopefully, them, too.

As it sweeps over us, age leads us to want to shrink the world around us; wrap ourselves more in isolation. A smaller world is an easier world. Fewer hassles. Less stress. Easier to control. Who doesn't want those things? I sure do. Engagement with others often is disruptive. It makes planning out one's day more difficult. With others part of the mix, one has to be willing to compromise, adjust, postpone things you want to do for yourself, think of things to talk about with others. As one ages, who wants to take on all those challenges? Not me so much. At least not all the time. Yet, with age, comes the realization that life is one compromise after another. Embracing the notion that even with all the colors in the world, there is much gray, too. Different perspectives. Different beliefs. Different ways of doing things. There are also fewer absolutes that trigger the inevitable concession that other ways of viewing life exist. Embracing that notion seems to be a prudent way to get through each day. Agreeing with the differences within life or even understanding them fully seems less important than simply acknowledging their presence. More and more I am convinced that people, generally, are not so much as interested in being acknowledged as right or correct as they are in being heard. These days I am trying to practice the act of conversational listening like never before. Wanna talk politics? Go for it! Tell me how you feel. I will do my best to see your perspective. If you want to know what I think, then fine. But if not, that is okay, too. Wanna talk sports? Bring it on. I have played enough in my lifetime to be a good audience. Same goes for movies. I have seen more than enough to be comfortable with sharing my likes and dislikes. But what about you? The need to air my views about most anything is declining as the willingness to let others air theirs is rising. I am thinking that is how it has been with much of my life. Does that make me comfortable in my own skin? Maybe. Would passive be a better description of me? No, I do not believe so. Not yet anyway. Perhaps, instead, I am on my way to becoming more compatible with life itself.

7

Still Walking

It began with a simple conversation. My cousin and I were talking on the phone. As we live in different states, we do not see each other as often as we would like. To change that—at least a little—I suggested that he and I should go on a big hike every year in some part of the country that would be fun to see and explore. He was immediately on board with that. That was 2008. After some back and forth, we decided that if we were going to do this, then we should start big. Grand Canyon here we come! July, 2009, we hiked down the Grand Canyon and spent the night at what is called the Phantom Ranch. Fascinating place. Run by very friendly people. Rustic environment. Beautiful surroundings. Anyone who refuses to stay in anything less ritzy than a Marriott should not go to the Phantom Ranch. But everyone else should give it a try. However, at least back then, you had to call nearly a year in advance for reservations. Getting there is also an adventure. You either hike or ride a horse. Either one is a challenge. Hiking more so. But much like life itself, the trek is well worth it.

In the months leading up to what my cousin and I termed "Debacle 1," we both began training in our own ways in anticipation of what we knew would be physically demanding. Still, we had not even left the comfort of our homes and already we were having a good time. Lots of conversation. Lots of joking. Loving put-downs. Much to our delight, the anticipation of the trip was exceeded by the trip itself. The Grand Canyon is as majestic as it is breathtaking. There is a unique stillness that emanates from the Canyon that highlights the power of this magnificent jewel of Mother Nature. For me, approaching it filled me with a high level of reverence. Taking that first step onto the trail on the Canyon's North Side was most memorable. Six hours later we were on the floor of the Canyon. In the hike down, my strategy was to conserve my water supply so as not to run out before reaching our destination. I went too far. Hours passed. About one mile from our camp site, I felt like I was going to collapse. I was dehydrated. Self-inflicted dehydration. Is that even possible? I plopped down on the ground without any desire to get back up. One would think the fact it was in the middle of summer and the temperature was over one hundred degrees would mean I would have been smart enough to drink more water than I did. Not me. At least not on that day. But as I still had a goodly supply to draw from, I slowly began to regain my energy as I drank my water. Not one of my better moments other than being a good teachable one. My cousin, I should note, was helpful in his usual irreverent yet caring way.

Finally, we made our way to the main campsite. Other hikers were there, of course, as was the staff, including several park rangers. The feeling of comradery among all of us made the atmosphere a most positive one. My cousin and I unloaded our back packs and began settling in for the remainder of the day. We would hike back up the Canyon the next day.

I am proud to say that we would replicate this memorable adventure on an annual basis through 2019 only at different locations. (Because of the COVID-19 pandemic, we did not do any hiking in 2020.) As the cliché goes, "nothing lasts forever," and we concluded our annual adventures in 2021, this time in Montana. During those years, our annual adventures ranged from the White Mountains of Vermont and the Bad Lands of South Dakota to trails in Alaska and, for us, great hikes along the Rockies. Multiple states and places in-between the east and west coasts. Great beauty. Great times. Bonding conversations. Talks about life, families, hopes, dreams, disappointments, life highlights. Also, our hikes have been filled with silence as much as dialogue. For me, they resurrected memories of my own walks decades earlier when I ventured to and from my favorite drug stores in my hometown community. My memories also include treks up and down main and side streets of towns where I have lived: Knoxville, Clarksville, Hagerstown, Glen Burnie, Fairfax, Woodlawn, and even Songdo, South Korea. One step after another in those neighborhoods that now comprise my history. And then there are the communities that I have visited, including ones in foreign lands in which I lived and/or traveled in Europe, Asia and North America. I realize that as much as they were all geared for purposes of exploration, each walk was also about me. Opportunities for me and my thoughts to catch-up and reminisce. Welcome new musings into a private well of contemplation, mentally grappling with whatever issues of the day found notable or troubling.

Walking. The common thread linking my youth and maturity. Those times of my life and all that I did in between them in my ongoing quest to seek knowledge, greater understanding, the acceptance of others and myself, growth, solitude, escape, wisdom, self-reflection, and courage. Collectively, they represent a key essence of me that I pursue and then strive to maintain. Pure contemplation is a big deal with me. Yes, I am a guy who likes to go for a walk. Not just for the exercise, however. Exercise is a bonus. Exercise is often the excuse I use to lose myself on-foot in my own reflections. When in what I call my "walking zone," I often have to remind myself to turn around. Walking helps me go mano a mano with my worries. Granted, at the finish of each walk the worries may not have necessarily vanished or been vanquished. But walking helps me give them the perspective I need so as not to give them so much power; not make them seem so formidable that I cannot contend with them. That is the superpower of worries—their perceived ability to make themselves seem bigger than they actually are. But like a bully, often when confronted, they can be faced down. Walking helped and helps me do that. Also, walking remains an opportunity to revisit my internal hall of mirrors. Here is me sad. Here is me angry. Over there I am joyful. Right behind me is a mirror where I look to be depressed. And then there are mirrors where I look confused and afraid and troubled and care-free and joyous and even confident. There are as many mirrors as I have emotions and feelings. They seem limitless and yet confined within the body and mind that is me.

Questions I raised way back when I was so young, I still raise and struggle with today. Have I been worthy of the great gift that is life? How about worthy of the regard of others? What is wrong with me? Nothing? Everything? What is right with me? Maybe a few things? Will I finally be able to embrace my normality and let go of fantasies of exceptionalism? On the other hand, maybe those fantasies are worth hanging onto a little while longer. When am I ever going to get better at opening myself up to others in ways that I feel emotionally and even intellectually safe? There must be a way—even now—when I can right the wrongs I have committed in my life as well as build on that which I have done well. Will what others think of me ever not be important to me? How come I never was able to reconcile wanting recognition with not wanting the spotlight? Age, of course, introduced new in-my-face questions into my repertoire. How can I be a better husband, father, grandfather, friend, person? Is there a way to achieve those goals without disappointing those I love too much? Adding it all up, would I have the courage of Tom Sawyer who, in one of his adventures, when the townspeople thought he was dead, sneaked into his own funeral service and got to hear what folks had to say about him? I am not sure I would be able to do that. It would not matter whether or not the comments were positive.

Funny. After all these years I am wrestling with many of the same questions that I did years before. Is that normal? Is this how it is with other grown-ups? I suppose one piece of good news is that maybe—just maybe—I have gained some insight into these self-directed inquiries. On the other hand, however, I am not sure if the fact the questions still remain completely unanswered is an indication that I have not made all that much progress in my life other than I am now taller, have grayer hair, have a few credit cards to deal with, and have to at least try and balance my checkbook from time to time. These questions, I concede, have served as guideposts in my journey through life. Instead of saying "Next Rest Stop, 20 Miles," they have served as reminders that every so often I need to pull-over and reflect. Add up my own personal score. Identify that which I need to change or adjust in my behavior and thinking or simply keep doing what I have been doing. Face that which I need to build on. Never mind how well I did in any particular areas of my life such as marriage, parenting, work, citizenship or intellectual growth. Together, they and other areas constitute much of my current reflections. The hard truth is, at times in each of them, I did nothing despite the fact my inner voice screamed at me to change course. My inner voice would cry out for me to be braver, be more open, be kinder, buckle down, be more mindful of others, keep smiling, keep listening, keep collecting reasons to be grateful, keep recognizing that my life is filled with potential—even now—keep focusing on the positive and not giving life's negatives any more power than they deserve. But to be fair, there are as many times, if not more, when I did listen to that voice. So, maybe it all balances out. Not totally sure. Perhaps the fact I remain able and willing to keep some sort of tally each day is the best thing of all. If nothing else, I believe it demonstrates my concession that I do not know all the answers to my life and that I am now at least smart enough to know that much. So, score one for me. When it comes to my own survival and quest for peace of mind, staying the course with periodic reviews demonstrates at least the beginning of my own, if not super power, then nugget of wisdom. So, here's to perseverance. Suiting up every day and ignoring that part of my inner voice that whispers, "Break time. Worry about being a better you tomorrow." With each less hair on my head, with each stiff joint, with each gap in memory, I still refuse to listen to that particular whisper. Perhaps, as it is with others, I am like Miguel de Cervantes' Don Quixote who follows a quest. In my case, my quest may not be as romantic or noble as striving to "defend the helpless and destroy the wicked," but nevertheless aims at doing more good than not.

Why the vigilance? That's an easy one. I owe too much to the people who helped bring me to this point in my life. My parents. My wife. My daughter. Family. Friends. Co-workers. Every one of you—to this day—walks with me. Regardless of whether I am on the Appalachian Trail, here in our neighborhood or in the frozen food section of the local grocery store, I recognize that my steps are not mine alone. With me on each step is every person who touched my heart and mind no matter if it was in a good or bad way. Like a recipe, I see so much of me as a mixing together of countless ingredients. I can only hope the result is pleasing to those with whom I continue to intersect. If not, then my only defense is, "Hey, I'm working on it." Tall order? Yes. Impossible? Probably. Worth the effort? You bet. Be the best version of me as it applies to others. Walking then, has evolved into my own private and personal lab where I strive to concoct the version that speaks to the standards for myself that enable me to move forward on this quest of mine.

If I had to lose one emotional characteristic which one would it be? Sense of humor? Anger? Empathy? Joy? Sadness? Can't say. One thing for sure, however, the ability to feel empathy would be a major loss for me. Being able to feel or sense the emotions of others helps me stay connected and provides me with perspective into what I might be feeling at any given time. "Yeah, I am upset, but what about them?" I do not wish my emotions to exist within a vacuum or without some sort of regard or relation to what others around me are experiencing. I do not want me to be all about me.

How about a physical ability or attribute? Which one of those would I part with? Vision? Hearing? Taste? Mobility? That is a tough one, too. Letting go of any part of me would be a dark day. Yet aging makes real the prospect of such a moment when I become less than what I was. The ying and yang of life: growth and diminishment. The difference for me and all of us is that often we are not given a choice. Our ability to remember begins packing its bags almost immediately after we are born until one day it is gone. Without warning, our ability to hear is diminished to the point when turning up the volume on the television set no longer works. Running to catch a bus? Not anymore. I will sit here and wait for the next one to arrive. And on and on. I can only hope that the physical, intellectual and emotional abilities and qualities I once possessed have been replaced or even enhanced by new ones. These would include the ability to be practical, place things in perspective, be more tolerant, place life's turns in a more realistic context so that I may continue to have some sort of viable coping skills as well as positive impact on others. Oliver Wendell Holmes, Sr. once said, "The young man knows the rules but the old man knows the exceptions." Moving forward, I strive to gain the kind of wisdom that recognizes the proper time for exceptions and the conviction to make them.

Acknowledgements

I can appreciate the challenge of deciding who to recognize when it comes to telling one's life story. Who do I single out? Who had a notable impact on my life to where they deserve special recognition? Obviously, there are some folks that are prominent. Forever they are like beautiful constellations in my personal sky. These men and women have and continue to make a positive difference in my being. I speak of close family members and dear friends. Thank you for being the best part of me and the role you keep playing in bringing out whatever good qualities I may have. When it comes to debt, I owe all of you much more than any of you may owe me.

It is difficult for me to think of most anyone who has not influenced me in some way. I freely admit that I have tried taking what I believe is the best of you and tried equally hard to make it part of my own persona. This goes for the few folks who I did not necessarily cotton to as well. The first-hand experience of what I deemed to be your negative qualities reinforced my idea of how not to be. So, to you, I also say, "Thank you."

I am blessed and grateful. Each day is a gift in large measure because of each of my encounters. Thanks for the oh-so fresh memories. As Amanda Gorman, the youngest inaugural presidential poet in the history of the United States observed, echoing a legend of uncertain origin: there are two wolves inside each of us, one that must be fought and one that must be fed. All that I know and have known helped me feed that part of me that strives to, in Gorman's words, "never fail."

As far as this book goes, I am thankful to those who shared their editorial expertise and friendly support, particularly Andrew Rouner and Hannah McLaughlin of George Mason University Press. What a treasure the two of you are! Without question, you raised the quality of my autobiography. Much like my life itself, you made it better. Thank you for being so selfless. And speaking of selfless individuals,

I must acknowledge my wife and life partner, Jo, daughter, Tracy, her husband, Robert, step-daughter Lori, and my super-duper granddaughter, Madison. Whatever bounce remains in my step is because of each of you.

About the Author

Following a half-century-long career in communication, Dr. Daniel Walsch is happily enjoying retirement with his wife, Jo. They reside in Northern Virginia. No pets for now. He is the author of an array of books on public relations and communication, several of which have been used as textbooks at institutions of higher learning throughout the United States. His writing efforts have also included a humor and children's book and a successful blog. While he will not say "no" to more writing projects, Dr. Walsch's primary goals include seeking to be the best he can be, remaining healthy, continuing to enjoy his family and friends, keep walking, and living to be at least one-hundred years of age.

www.ingramcontent.com/pod-product-compliance
Lightning Source LLC
Chambersburg PA
CBHW051606170426
43196CB00038B/2949

www.ingramcontent.com/pod-product-compliance
Lightning Source LLC
Chambersburg PA
CBHW051606170426
43196CB00038B/2951